Courage
— AND —
RESILIENCE

A BOOMER'S STORY OF
REINVENTION, TRIUMPH, AND THE
ENTREPRENEURIAL ROLLER COASTER

MICHAEL W.G. BERMAN

Table of Contents

Dedication

For my Mother, Frances, and Father, Jeremiah, from where I got my Strength, Tenacity, and Courage. Thank you!

Thank you, my life partner, for Lucy. Your unconditional love, encouragement, emotional substance, and unquestioning support have been my nourishment and beacon for renewed love. You are the wind beneath my wings and the love of my Life!

Jen and Rob, your unconditional love is such a blessing. Not enough words tell you how much you both mean to me. Stephanie, your entrepreneurial spirit, courage, and tenacity serve you well and make me proud.

Carol and Diane, your generosity, support, and unwavering friendships are Treasured Gifts.

"As Idowu Koyenikan wisely said, "We do not get to choose how we start in life." Indeed, the circumstances of our birth and upbringing are often predetermined and beyond our control. Yet, how we choose to move forward truly defines our path. "When you are old enough to start making decisions, many things in your life are already in place. It's crucial, therefore, that you focus on the future, the only thing you can control,"

Also By, Michael W.G. Berman

Baby Boomers Guide to the Creator Economy
Blueprint Series Vol 1 Leveraging Social Media
Blueprint Series Vol 2 Understanding E-Commerce
Blueprint Series Vol 3 Unlocking Your Potential
Tomorrow Still Waits - A Tale of Hope and Humanity

ACKNOWLEDGEMENTS

So many people have positively impacted my life. Many are from my past, some of whom I have referred to in this memoir. Uncle Lloyd, Uncle Ira, Aunt Gaby, Stewart, and Cheryl. I am blessed to have these people in "my movie." I appreciate your impact on me. To my support system. Thank you. Bob Hidell, Stan Sidman, Wayne Mogel, Anthony Damore, Neil Berman, Thomas Shane, Peter Colgan, and Michael Briansky.

Anything Is Possible

Anything is possible in a world of infinite potential,
Where thoughts can turn to reality
And dreams can be made actual.
Presents fade, but presence stays,
A gift more precious than gold,
So jump in with no safety net,
And let your heart unfold.
Embrace the unknown, take a chance,
If anything is possible,
With courage in your heart and soul,
You'll find the strength to conquer all."
Michael W.G. Berman

Introduction

Resilience Reborn

As I stood in my office conference room that fateful morning in 2013, I had no idea my life was about to be turned upside down. At 65, when most of my peers were settling into retirement, I faced a personal crisis that would shake the foundation of my world.

In a few hours, the life I had built over 35 years - my marriage, business, and sense of identity - came crashing down around me. I was handed a restraining order and told to leave my home and everything I knew. That night, I slept in my car, wondering how I had gone from a successful entrepreneur to a homeless, jobless, and soon-to-be divorced man.

The months that followed were some of the darkest of my life. But through the pain and uncertainty, I found a resilience and determination I never knew I possessed. I knew that my journey, however difficult, was far from over.

In this memoir, I'll take you on a rollercoaster ride through the ups and downs of my life as a Boomer entrepreneur. From my early days growing up in the shadow of my parents' Holocaust experience to my first forays into the business world, I'll share the lessons, triumphs, and failures that have shaped my path.

You'll be by my side as I navigate the challenges of raising a family while building multiple successful ventures. You'll witness the dizzying heights of success and the gut-wrenching lows of loss and betrayal. And you'll see how, repeatedly, I've picked myself up, dusted myself off, and found the courage to reinvent myself and start anew.

Through it all, we'll explore the key themes that have defined my journey: resilience in the face of adversity, the power of relationships and mentorship, the importance of adaptability in an ever-changing world, and the unwavering belief in the potential for growth and transformation at any age.

Whether you're an entrepreneur or simply someone who appreciates a good comeback story, I invite you to join me on this wild ride. Together, we'll laugh, cry, and discover that anything is possible with enough grit, determination, and nerve.

So buckle up and get ready for the adventure of a lifetime. It's time to redefine what becoming a Boomer entrepreneur in the 21st century means.

A Note on Dates, Chronology, and Anecdotes

In sharing my life story, I've done my best to recount events and experiences as accurately as possible. However, given the passage of time and the inherent fallibility of memory, some of the dates and sequences mentioned in this memoir may need to be revised.

In sharing these anecdotes, I aim to give you, the reader, a richer and more nuanced understanding of my experiences, challenges, and triumphs. Each story is a puzzle piece, contributing to the larger picture of my entrepreneurial journey and the lessons I've learned.

Ultimately, I hope that by sharing my journey - both the highs and the lows, the victories and the setbacks - I will inspire and empower you to embrace your entrepreneurial path with courage, resilience, and a steadfast commitment to your dreams. The road may be winding and the destination uncertain, but I promise you, the journey itself is the most rewarding adventure of all."

-Redefining Retirement in the 21st Century -

Through my triumphs and failures, I've discovered that success is not about avoiding obstacles but developing the tenacity to overcome them. By focusing on the future and embracing the power of change, we can all write unique stories of achievement and personal growth.

As you read through these pages, I hope my experiences inspire you to dream big, face your fears, and never give up on your aspirations. **Remember, your past does not dictate your future. You can shape your destiny, one courageous decision at a time.**

Rather than dwelling on mistakes, turn the page, get off the ride, and learn from them. Guilt and regret hinder progress; moving forward with newfound wisdom is critical. This memoir imparts wisdom from my journey, blending personal experience with timeless truths about the power of the process of elimination in understanding oneself. Identifying and eliminating negative influences paves the way for a more authentic and fulfilling life.

The heart of this book is defining success on your terms and embracing the process of becoming the author of your own life. I invite you to join me on this journey of self-discovery, where we will shape our narratives together for a more authentic and purposeful path forward.

A Boomer Perspective

We boomers are always talking about writing a book, aren't we? Well, I'm doing it. It's time to take a good, hard look at my life—from where I started to where I am now. This self-reflection is not easy. It can be downright brutal, dredging up the past and all. Each of our journeys is unique.

For my younger readers, some of you may have a misconception about us boomers. You might think, 'Oh, those boomers are all just a bunch of retirees.' Well, let me tell you, that's far from the truth. Thanks to better healthcare and healthier habits, many of us 70-somethings are fitter than our parents were in their 50s and 60s. Age is not an excuse and this idea that everyone over 65 is ready to kick back and relax? It's a myth. Most boomers don't want to retire.

That's one of the main reasons I'm writing this book - to actively inspire the next generation of entrepreneurs, the ones riding the wave of this 'creator economy' thing. Some stories in this book will ignite a fire under those budding business owners and innovators from every generation. Because let me tell you, the best is yet to come, no matter how many birthdays you have had.

So OK, Boomers and all my dear readers- let's dive in. It's time to trace my steps, unravel my journey, and see what life's lessons offer. One thing's for sure - I won't let age hold me back. There needs to be more left to explore.

Growth and self-realization are beautiful things, regardless of when they occur in a person's life. People can learn and share valuable lessons from their hardships. I have always valued having mentors in business and life. Because I know how important mentors were to me at such a young age, I've always promised myself that if I could offer my advice and wisdom someday, I would.

Looking back, one of my greatest strengths has been my intuitive ability to spot changes and patterns and leverage my creative thinking to devise novel solutions. It's a skill I've honed in on, and that is - having the courage to seek answers, even when unconventional.

I relish the challenge of achieving the "impossible." There's a thrill when Someone tells you something can't be done, only to prove the naysayers wrong through sheer determination and innovative thinking. This mindset has been a driving force throughout my life, pushing me to explore uncharted territory and discover unconventional paths forward.

I've come to understand that this innate quality, this desire to do the seemingly impossible, is a large part of what makes me who I am. It's not just a skill but a core part of my identity—something that drives me crazy in the best possible way. Through all the twists and turns life has thrown my way, this restless, creative spirit has kept me going and fueled my persistence in the face of adversity.

As I look to the future, I'm excited to continue harnessing this intuitive ability to navigate new challenges. There is always more uncharted territory to explore, more "impossibilities" waiting to be made possible. I can't wait to share the lessons I've learned to inspire others who might be told their dreams are not worth reaching because

I know from experience that the impossible is always within— go with the right mindset and determination.

- **Lessons Learned from Early Experience**

This book you hold is a partial account of my life journey. Instead, it's a glimpse into the successes, speed bumps, and traumatic experiences that have shaped me into who I am today. Each triumph and each trial, no matter how difficult, has served a purpose in strengthening my character, sharpening my wisdom, and equipping me to handle life's responsibilities.

Reflecting on my path, I've embraced the belief that even the most devastating events happen for a reason. This sentiment is echoed in the wisdom of Rabbi Harold Kushner's seminal work, "Why Bad Things Happen to Good People." *In it, he posits that suffering is neither a punishment nor a test from a vengeful deity. Instead, it is simply a part of the human experience - an unavoidable consequence of living in an imperfect world.*

What matters most, Kushner argues, is *"how we choose to respond to life's challenges. Do we succumb to bitterness and despair or summon the courage to find meaning and growth amidst the darkness?"* I've sought to embody this philosophy throughout my life's journey.

Adversity is not a divine punishment nor a trial to be endured but rather an inevitable part of the human experience. As I've navigated the ups and downs of my entrepreneurial journey, I've come to embrace this fundamental truth - that suffering is not the result of cosmic retribution but simply the unavoidable consequence of living in an imperfect world.

I've learned the key to how we choose to respond to life's challenges. Do we succumb to bitterness and despair or summon the courage to find meaning and growth amidst the darkness? It was a lesson brought into sharp focus when I faced the devastating loss of my father at the tender age of 15.

I can still vividly recall the moment the news reached me—the crushing weight of grief and the overwhelming sense of helplessness. In the following weeks, I was thrust into the unfamiliar role of "liquidator," tasked with closing down my father's factory. Navigating the complex web of legal and financial matters while grappling with the hollowness of my tragedy was a surreal experience.

Yet, even in the depths of that sorrow, I discovered an inner wellspring of resilience. Rather than succumbing to bitterness, I channeled my energy into learning the intricacies of the business world, soaking up every lesson like a sponge. It was a painful but transformative process that would ultimately forge the foundations of my entrepreneurial journey.

Time and again, I've faced circumstances that threatened to break me - the acrimonious divorce that left me financially and emotionally decimated, the business ventures that crumbled in the face of unforeseen obstacles. But I've dug deep each time, drawing strength from an unwavering belief that these trials were not merely random misfortunes but opportunities to evolve and become more resilient, empathetic, and intentional about the path forward.

By embracing adversity as a catalyst for growth, I've learned to view even the darkest of circumstances through a lens of possibility. The setbacks were not punishments but lessons—painful, perhaps, but ultimately fortifying. They forced me to cultivate an adaptable mindset, become a creative problem-solver, and never take success for granted.

As I look to the future, I do so with a deep sense of gratitude and purpose. The challenges I've endured have imbued me with an unshakable conviction: that there is meaning to be found in even the darkest circumstances and that every obstacle presents an opportunity to become a better version of myself. I want to impart this hard-won philosophy to those who read these pages - that even when life deals with you, a cruel hand can transform adversity into strength and *find light in the darkness.*

So, let this book be a testament to the resilience of the human spirit, to the belief that no matter how steep the climb, the summit is always within reach. Ultimately, it is not the destination that matters most but the journey itself—the lessons learned, the character forged, and the insights gained along the way.

I lost count of how many times I thought I had a golden goose in my hand, only for the number to change to zero. It's all a part of the entrepreneurial journey.

Entrepreneurship starts when you recognize the potential of a simple idea. You make it happen through a continuous work process guided by a business plan and the resources you need to make it successful.

In his book Innovation and Entrepreneurship, Peter Drucker said, "*Entrepreneurship is neither a science nor an art.*" *It is a practice. It is a knowledge base. But in all practices, like medicine, for instance, or engineering, knowledge in entrepreneurship is a means to an end.*"

Building a company requires creativity, vision, intuition, imagination, and inspiration. These are all Supported by the founder's passion and courage, which are intangible assets.

In today's world, where everything seems to have been built, tried, and thought of, you, as an entrepreneur, need to have a sparkling idea that will make you build something big, beautiful, and new. The mental process of being stimulated to launch a startup has much to do with creativity. It is called inspiration.

I love this quote from Dan Pink on 21st-Century Thinking.

"*The last few decades have belonged to a certain kind of person with a certain kind of mind-programmers who can crank code, lawyers who can craft contracts, and MBAs who can crunch numbers.*" *But the key to the kingdom is changing hands. The future belongs to a very different kind of person with a different type of mind—creators and empathizers, pattern recognizers, and meaning makers. These artists, inventors, designers, storytellers, caregivers, and big-picture thinkers—will now reap society's richest rewards and share its greatest joys. "*

"Pink's words struck a chord with me, affirming my belief in the power of creativity and innovation. As an entrepreneur, I've always sought to embody the qualities he describes - to be a creator, an empathizer, a pattern recognizer, and a meaning maker. This passage reinforced my commitment to leveraging these skills not only to build successful ventures but to make a positive impact on the world."

To a large extent, entrepreneurs are similar to novelists, sculptors, or painters because they invent and design something that did not exist before. They embed a piece of themselves in what they have created. And just as great artists create masterpieces, occasionally inspired founders create startup works of art. ***This is exactly how I perceive myself to be!***

My enthusiasm for life comes from taking chances and being bold to face the consequences. Like a roller coaster, these highs and lows delight me about my journey. My readiness to fail has given me the capacity to prevail. I've been discouraged many times and wanted to quit, but I'm glad I stuck with it and followed my path. I've been in business for over 50 years.

This willingness to fall flat on my face has paradoxically given me the capability to succeed. Some people choose to complete laborious tasks because they have no other option, but starting a business can be challenging. As an entrepreneur, I've had to learn virtually every aspect of running a business - from bookkeeping and accounting to marketing, leadership, and scaling. It was a steep learning curve, but one I embraced wholeheartedly, as the freedom to be my boss and pursue my passions without constraints has always been the ultimate prize.

Even when I've succeeded, there has been no shortage of failures - curb cuts, marketing miscalculations, miscommunications, and technologies that seemed constant. But I've come to see each obstacle as an opportunity in disguise. Each time I've faced an unfamiliar challenge, I've had to dig deep, get creative, and find a solution, even if it wasn't the right one right away. That's the nature of entrepreneurship - you can't expect to have all the answers or be an expert in every domain. But that's also what makes it so thrilling and rewarding. With each new hurdle, I've grown more assertive, resilient, and adept at navigating the unpredictable waters of business ownership.

The unique amalgamation of skills, knowledge, and instincts I've developed over the years—my "personal domain information"—sets me apart. It allows me to see opportunities where others might only see dead ends and to problem-solve in ways that defy convention. I hope to pass this entrepreneurial spirit and relentless pursuit of freedom to the next generation of trailblazers.

The journey has undoubtedly been filled with failures and speed bumps. Still, those moments have forged my character, sharpened my abilities, and instilled an unshakable belief that anything is possible with enough grit and creativity—the true essence of entrepreneurial life.

Over the years, I've learned that I want to spend my time and energy on something other than building someone else's dream. I crave the freedom to shape the entire process according to my vision. That's why I decided to strike out on my own, to create my enterprises from the ground up. I did not have all the answers, but I can promise I gave it my absolute best shot. After all, I'd rather fail on my terms than succeed in serving someone else's agenda.

While there's a wealth of information for aspiring entrepreneurs, many people are stubbornly set on doing things their way, regardless of the evidence or expert advice. They think they've cracked the code and found the secret path to riches and fame. More often than not, they're sorely mistaken.

That's why I've learned to trust my instincts and rely on the practical knowledge I've gained through trial and error. There's no substitute for real-world experience when the rubber meets the road. And I've got that in spades.

The overarching lesson I've taken away is to always appreciate the power of self-determination, of refusing to settle for someone else's vision of success. Sure, the road is filled with setbacks and failures, but that's all part of the journey, the price of admission to the club of true innovators and trailblazers. And you know what? I wouldn't have it any other way.

While working for someone else is perfectly acceptable, becoming an entrepreneur is the only way for me to truly take charge of my future. I chose this path to experience greater freedom, to wake up every day and work for myself, which is how I define freedom, and to have a better work-life balance.

PART I

FOUNDATIONS

I'm American-made. I benefited from being born in a time and place of unprecedented prosperity, with many advantages. These are my "framing" memories (where my dreaming started) and reflecting on how lucky I was to grow up middle class, Jewish, living in Newton, Mass, during the 50s and 60s (suburban Boston, with an all-access pass to New England). I had two great role models to give me a foundation for the future. To be noted, it was a period in time when women were emerging in a male-dominated world.

1. A Mother's Legacy: Lessons in Resilience and Determination

Growing up, I witnessed firsthand the power of resilience and determination in adversity. My mother, a fiery redhead with a spirit to match, embodied these qualities as she carved her path in a world that often underestimated women. In 1962, she fearlessly opened her art gallery in Newtonville, MA, despite the challenges of being a female entrepreneur in a male-dominated world.

Her tenacity and courage extended beyond her business ventures. As the first woman President of the American Jewish Congress, she shattered glass ceilings and paved the way for future generations of female leaders. Balancing her ambitions with supporting my father's business taught me the value of hard work, adaptability, and the importance of chasing one's dreams.

My mom took me to many live performances by famous musicians, which I was in awe of. This is where I formed my love of reading, jazz, and film. Mom was a movie buff with a fondness for foreign-language films. When we traveled to NYC and Washington, DC, Mom purposely took us to art galleries and museums.

She always pointed out famous architectural gems and beautiful gardens and structures. She sparked my interest in film, history, and nature. I got my appreciation for food, cooking, and good health from my mother. I remember early on when Mom would prepare Shabbat dinner for Friday night. She ensured I was enrolled in Hebrew school and made Judaism a part of my life. Looking back, I see how much my mother's resilience shaped me. Watching her rebuild her life after the devastating loss of my father, I learned that no matter how hard you get knocked down, you always have the strength to get back up. That lesson would become my guiding light as I navigated the ups and downs of entrepreneurship.

-Anecdote: Mom and Hilda

My mom was always taking a course or reading a book. Mom and Her best friend Hilda were antiwar activists who burned my draft card at the draft board on Austin Street in Newton Corner (I had a low "lottery number," and she was horrified I would be going into battle). I remember seeing my draft card on the front page of the Newton Graphic newspaper being burned. (I ended up serving stateside at Fort Sam Houston, in San Antonio, Texas (a war story for another day)

My mother's involvement in the anti-war movement profoundly impacted me. Watching her passionately stand up for her beliefs, even in the face of opposition, taught me the importance of speaking truth to power and fighting for your beliefs.

Mom and Hilda also sponsored and opened a "pop-up" anti-war and women's rights information center. During this time, I recall a conversation with her in which she encouraged me to dream big, which led me down my path or journey! "Fighting" for "peace" (an oxymoron) and equal rights for women left an indelible mark on my mind. Speaking out for women's rights and anti-war activists was a big deal.

Mom's life takes its turn.

What happened to my mom and the family was the tragic and sudden passing of my dad in July of 1964. My family was fractured, and my mom was only 37 with three kids. I was 15.5. After mourning this life-changing loss, she started to study to become a family therapist. Exposing me to "psychology" and introducing me to the world of self-help and psychotherapy.

Over the following years, she built a robust private practice focused on helping women and couples navigate their lives. Mom also led by example and was always volunteering, embracing the idea of being of service. Her study and practice motivated me to major in both business and psychology. As my life and my sibling's lives went on, we had kids, etc.; during this time, she enjoyed her six grandchildren and always gave them a gift for their birthdays or holidays related to art or music.

As mom turned 82, I saw a rapid decline in her health as she had to let go of her independent living and go to an assisted living situation. So, for six years, we witnessed her eventual demise.

So, a part of the untold story was that mom also suffered from deep depression due to early childhood trauma. Since her passing, I have been able to reflect and see her pain and depression and understand how it affected her and influenced our mother-son relationship, particularly in light of my dad's passing, from which she never recovered. (A story for another day.)

My mom and all of us were helpless as to how to navigate the diseases of depression and dementia. This was heartbreaking and very hard. She passed away at age 88.

-Honoring My Mother's Legacy: Helping the less fortunate and easing suffering.

Reflecting on my mother's passing has been a profound and profoundly motivating experience. In the wake of her loss, I felt compelled to find a solution - a way to help alleviate the isolation, anxiety, pain, and depression that so many people, especially those living in nursing homes, face daily.

My mother's struggles with these challenges had a profound impact on me, and I realize now that the "seed" of my current pursuits was planted long ago, rooted in her experience. As I've navigated the landscape of life after her death, I've been able to see just how much she has informed who I am today - both as a person and in the direction of my professional work.

The lessons she taught me and the resilience she modeled in the face of adversity have driven my efforts to make a difference in the lives of the lonely and suffering. I've seen firsthand the devastating toll that isolation can take and how it can erode one's sense of purpose and joy. And I'm determined to change that narrative, to provide a glimmer of hope and connection for those who need it most.

Through my work, I've had the privilege of witnessing the profound impact that technology, specifically virtual reality, can have in alleviating the burdens of loneliness and depression in nursing home settings. It's as if my mother's struggles have become the catalyst for solutions that I'm now able to bring to fruition, honoring her memory in the most meaningful way.

Each breakthrough, each smile I see on a resident's face experiencing the immersive, therapeutic power of VR, is a testament to the lasting influence of my mother's life. With all its challenges and triumphs, her journey has become the foundation upon which I build my path forward. And I know, without a doubt, that she is watching over me, urging me onward, proud of the difference I'm making in the lives of those who, like her, have faced the darkness of isolation.

As I continue to navigate this journey, I do so with a deep sense of purpose and gratitude. My mother's legacy has become my own, a driving force that propels me to reach higher, innovate more boldly, and never give up in the pursuit of easing the suffering of others. In honoring her memory, I find the strength to overcome any obstacle, make her proud, and create a brighter future for those who need it most.

I am forever grateful for my mother's unconditional love, education, sharing of joy and enthusiasm, and passion for life; she taught me so much. She told me to dream. To have big dreams! "Trust yourself, hold onto your dreams, and don't let anybody steal your shine."

Lessons In Resilience and Determination

Watching my mother navigate the complexities of entrepreneurship and leadership, I learned that success is not about having a smooth path but **the resilience to overcome obstacles and the courage to take risks.** Her example ignited a spark within me, laying the foundation for my entrepreneurial journey and teaching me that anything is possible with determination and grit. While my mother's tenacity and creativity inspired my entrepreneurial drive, my father's unwavering work ethic and keen business sense would also shape my journey."

2. Coming of Age in the Sixties: The Influence of a Changing World

As I reflect on my formative years, I can't help but recognize the profound influence that the cultural shift of the 1960s had on shaping my worldview. Growing up in the relative calm and conformity of 1950s suburban Boston, I was suddenly thrust into a decade of upheaval, social unrest, and a burgeoning counterculture movement that would leave an indelible mark on my psyche.

The civil rights struggle, the anti-war protests, and the explosion of art, music, and free-spirited experimentation swirled around me, stirring a sense of restlessness and a hunger for something more than The comfortable middle-class existence I had known. My mother's activism and willingness to challenge the status quo further stoked the flames of my curiosity and desire for change. As I navigated the turbulent waters of the 1960s, my father's guidance and example would provide a steady anchor amidst the sea of change.

58 Prescott St Newtonville- Where I grew up

3. Jeremiah M.G. Berman: A Fathers Guiding Light

My father's influence was pivotal in shaping my entrepreneurial spirit. As a World War II veteran, he embodied hard work, dedication, and integrity - qualities that would become the foundation of my approach to business. His keen business acumen and unwavering work ethic set a powerful example for me to follow.

"Lessons in Integrity and Hard Work"

As I look back on my life, some of my most cherished memories stem from my earliest years growing up alongside my beloved father. His boundless enthusiasm and creative spirit were infectious, igniting a spark within me that has continued to burn brightly throughout my journey.

I vividly recall the times I would accompany him to work, marveling at how he effortlessly connected with people and used his smarts and business acumen—it was like a dance, and I was mesmerized. Those outings fueled my entrepreneurial journey.

Some of my fondest recollections are of the winter wonderlands we would construct in our backyard or skating at the local pond, which would help us build towering snow forts or sandcastles on Nantasket Beach. Dad was always so proud of me for shoveling the driveway so he could get the car in the garage when he got home from work. My dad built a dark room in the basement to process our photos. I remember the awe of seeing the photo paper slowly have a beautiful image coming alive. Those moments that have remained Intact in my memory are a testament to the power of quality time spent with a parent who cherished creating magical experiences. I vividly remember times sailing in Marblehead Harbor and being with my dad.

I now view my life's trajectory through the lens of these early formative years. My father's unwavering support and willingness to nurture my curiosities and indulge my imaginative tendencies laid the groundwork for the person I would become. The lessons I learned from my father about honesty, hard work, and entrepreneurship would serve as a compass as I navigated the challenges and opportunities ahead.

-Anecdote: A Wow Moment

It was a pivotal moment with my father that genuinely cemented the values of honesty and integrity in my entrepreneurial spirit. I remember a business trip we took together to the G.H. Bass shoe factory in Wilton, Maine. My father noticed that the new computer system that Bass had implemented had mistakenly issued a check for significantly more than what he owed. He immediately brought the error to their attention and returned the check. It was a substantial amount of money for those times.

George Bass's reaction left an indelible mark on my young mind. He expressed his deep admiration and respect for my father's honesty. This experience taught me that integrity and transparency are the cornerstones of any successful business relationship.

-Anecdote Formative Moment Behind the Wheel

This lighthearted moment with my father was a testament to his trust and confidence in me, even at 14. As we drove back to Boston, he surprised me by letting me take the wheel of his 1963 Chrysler New Yorker. I eagerly accepted the opportunity, thrilled by the responsibility.

However, as I navigated the highway, I saw Dad had fallen asleep. I am sure he was tired from getting up so early and caught a quick nap. I soon found myself surrounded by traffic, trying to figure out how to operate the brakes properly. In a slight panic, I gently nudged my father awake and asked for guidance. His eyes widened as he quickly realized the precarious situation and promptly took back control of the car.

Though it was a tense moment, we laughed about the incident afterward. My father made me promise not to share the story with my mother, and I realized the importance of being adaptable and thinking quickly on my feet - skills that would prove invaluable throughout my entrepreneurial journey. This experience also reinforced the value of having mentors and guides to turn to when facing new challenges and uncertainties.

As I explored my passions further, I discovered they were more than just hobbies; they were a calling. I felt a deep sense of purpose and fulfillment when creating a new project, capturing moments, and telling stories through the lens. Perhaps most importantly, the lessons I learned about honesty and integrity from my father became the guiding principles that would shape my entrepreneurial journey.

4. Foreshadowing the Future: Learning to Embrace Change

-Sudden death

It now seems the universe was trying to prepare me for the devastating loss of my father, though, of course, you can never truly prepare for sudden death. Retrospectively, the untimely passing of my beloved family dog, followed by my grandfather's death just a few weeks later, appears to have been part of a larger pattern - a sequence of events foreshadowing the tragedy that was to come.

That summer, when I was fifteen, was a season of profound loss and disorienting change. Losing my father so suddenly, so unexpectedly, shattered the very foundation of my world. At an age when most boys were worried about getting their learner's permit or asking a girl to the movies, I found myself grappling with grief, confusion, and an overwhelming sense of responsibility.

The days following Dad's passing were a blur of hushed conversations, sad faces, and the sickening realization that nothing would ever be the same. As I stood in his factory, surrounded by the machines and materials that had been his life's work, I felt the weight of his absence like a physical ache in my chest. The once-vibrant space now felt hollow, a painful reminder of all that had been lost.

At 15.5, I was between the world of childhood and the looming demands of adulthood. While my friends enjoyed the carefree days of summer break, I was thrust into the unfamiliar "liquidator" role, a title far too heavy for my young shoulders. I stumbled through the unfamiliar legal jargon and financial statements, desperately trying to make sense of a world turned upside down.

But even amid this pain and uncertainty, I could feel the stirrings of something new within me - a flicker of resilience, a determination to honor my father's legacy and forge my path. Working alongside my

Uncle Ira in the leather business, I began to see glimmers of possibility amidst the darkness. The seeds of my entrepreneurial spirit, planted long ago by my father's example, began to take root and grow.

That summer was a crucible, a trial by fire that tested me in ways I never could have imagined. But it was also a turning point when I discovered the depths of my strength and the boundless potential ahead. As I emerged from the shadows of loss, I carried with me the indelible imprint of my father's love, the unwavering support of my family, and a newfound sense of purpose that would guide me through the challenges and triumphs to come."

Looking back, I can see how my father's profound loss shaped me into the person I am today. It taught me valuable lessons about resilience, adaptability, and the importance of pursuing one's passions in adversity. These lessons have remained with me throughout my entrepreneurial journey, guiding my decision-making and fueling my determination to succeed in the face of any obstacle. Adaptability was the name of the game in those early years. From high school hijinks to the Army Reserves to my Jamaican adventures, I was constantly learning to roll with the punches and make the most of whatever life threw my way. Little did I know, those early experiences prepared me for the rollercoaster ride of entrepreneurship, where the ability to pivot and adapt would be my greatest asset."

-The Seeds of Resilience

My parents left an indelible mark on me, their influences shaping the person I've become. I inherited a deep reverence for the natural world and an eye for capturing its beauty through the lens of a camera. I gained an openness of spirit and a willingness to approach life (and others) without preconceived notions or prejudice.

But the most profound legacy they've gifted me is an innate drive to dream big and bring those dreams to life. This quality has been both a blessing and a curse, pushing me to achieve more than I ever thought possible while setting me up for the occasional heartbreaks and failures.

Yet, this unrelenting ambition, this refusal to be constrained by conventional Thinking, has come to define me. It has inspired me to forge my path and create opportunities where none seemed to exist. I hope to pass on this spirit to future generations, a testament to the power of vision, determination, and the courage to chase the impossible.

So, as I look to the future, I do so with a profound sense of gratitude for the foundations laid by my parents. Their influence has become the bedrock upon which I've built my life's work - a life dedicated to dreaming big and seeing those dreams come to fruition, no matter the obstacles that may arise. It's a legacy I'm proud to carry forward that will continue to inspire me long after they're gone.

Even as the years have passed and life has thrown its fair share of curveballs my way, I find solace in revisiting those precious childhood memories. They remind me of the resilience and creativity that has continuously resided within me—a wellspring forged through my father's love, guidance, and example. That foundation has sustained me through the triumphs and tribulations that have since defined my journey.

As I stepped into the next chapter of my life, I carried with me the indelible imprint of my parent's love, the unwavering support of my family, and a newfound sense of purpose that would guide me through the challenges and triumphs to come.

As I navigate the uncharted waters of life, I do so with profound gratitude. The moments that have shaped me, the lessons that have molded me—the gifts that keep giving, reminders that even in the darkest times, there is light to be found in the cherished memories we hold dear.

-Anecdote: Reserved Parking - Memories of Boston in the 50'and 60s

As I entered the business world, I found myself drawing upon the invaluable lessons and examples set by my father. His entrepreneurial spirit and strong work ethic had left an indelible mark on my young mind, and I was eager to follow in his footsteps. My dad was a WWII Veteran. Until his passing, his influences showed up in me in so many ways. So many people say I look like him, walk like him, and have great energy!

During my first exposure to work or business, I was fortunate to have had a family of Entrepreneurs as models to learn from and what career path I would take. My dad's brothers, Lloyd and Ira, were entrepreneurs, as were my mother's parents, who owned a retail store selling high-end leather handbags for women. I had a lot of models to observe while I was impressionable!

I have fond, unforgettable memories and values, of which I will share a few.

-Reserved Parking

One of my most cherished memories of my father's business was his reserved parking space outside his office at 52-54 South Street in Boston. The sign "Jeremiah Berman Company, Reserved Parking" symbolized his success and dedication. Little did I know that years later, I would find myself with my reserved parking spot, just around the corner from where my father's had been. It was a poignant reminder of the legacy he had left behind and the path I was forging for myself.

From an early age, I was exposed to the business world through my dad's work, which opened my eyes to the diverse tapestry of people and cultures that make up our society. This exposure instilled a deep sense of openness and acceptance towards others, regardless of their background or beliefs.

Growing up, I had the privilege of interacting with people from various ethnic backgrounds, and it was through these interactions that I learned the importance of equality and non-prejudice. I realized that everyone has a unique story and that our differences should be celebrated, not feared or marginalized. This realization has become a core part of my being, guiding my personal and professional relationships.

Working alongside my father's employees, Louis Greenberg, Clarence Bayliss, and Pat Ronka, I gained invaluable insights into the business world. These men, hailing from the North End and South Boston, taught me the importance of hard work, street smarts, and building solid relationships. Their lessons and the skills I developed while talking to the "Bookie" at the Essex Coffee Shop: a guy with a crooked tie, a receding hairline, and bushy eyebrows. I observed people slipping a folded paper with some bills into his pocket with the betting slips. This was a part of my entrepreneurial education.

Now, at 75 years old, I can look back on my life with a deep sense of gratitude for the lessons I've learned and the experiences I've had. My early exposure to diversity, commitment to equality and non-prejudice, and Jewish upbringing have all contributed to the person I am today.

These values have guided me through challenges and triumphs and helped me build meaningful relationships with people from all walks of life. As I continue my journey, I remain committed to living a life of purpose, guided by openness, acceptance, and spiritual growth.

Downtown was considered very safe during the early '60s. My parents gave me a lot of freedom as a very young boy. I walked downtown, crossing and picking up hot dogs for fifteen cents each at "Joe and Nemos." I remember standing in the store with its large open picture windows and watching the bustle of people going to Filene's Basement and Jordan Marsh.

The Leather District (Essex Street) had the longest L-street-shaped bar in Boston. It had a front door on Atlantic Ave and another doorway on Essex St. The bar was massive. Every Friday when I was able to work) It was my job to go out to get Sub Sandwiches. The subs were huge and cost .75. The Lobster roll was giant for $1. I was fortunate to walk everywhere and explore the Italian North End, Chinatown, and the old waterfront now known as the Seaport District. Fast forward to today, a parent would be put in jail if they allowed a 10-year-old to roam the stress of Boston unsupervised.

Curiosity is a muscle that needs to be exercised!

As I moved forward in my career, this "Freedom" to explore sparked my "CURIOSITY" ("my curious nature") and became part of what continues shaping my career path as an Entrepreneur. This "FREEDOM" had shaped me into the entrepreneur I was becoming, and I was determined to honor their legacy through my successes and contributions.

Part II

The Journey Begins

As I embarked on my entrepreneurial journey, I was drawn to three passions that would shape my life: music, photography, and film. These creative pursuits allowed me to express myself, tell stories, and connect with the world. From the challenges I faced to the triumphs I achieved, my story is a testament to the enduring power of hard work, resilience, and wisdom passed down from generation to generation.

My love for these mediums was ignited by both of my parents, who introduced me to the arts at a young age, exposing me to a rich tapestry of creative expression. Through their guidance and encouragement, I developed a keen eye for beauty and a deep appreciation for the power of storytelling. I continue to ingest volumes of eclectic music. It always soothes my soul. To this day, I have a massive music library. I love to have music on when doing creative work, as it helps keep me "in flow," especially when I'm driving my car, and I can play it as loudly as possible!

As I explored these passions further, I discovered they were more than just hobbies; they were a calling. I felt a deep sense of purpose and fulfillment when creating ideas for projects or stories, capturing moments, and telling stories through the lens.

1. High School-The Army-Jamaica-My Unconventional Path to Adulthood

OK, junior and senior year of high school was a shit show. I had my dad's Chrysler. I had a connection (Gilbert, our cleaning lady's son) at Newtonville Liquor, and every Friday afternoon, I took orders from my classmates, drove the Chrysler to the back of the store, went in the front door, paid, and walked out with a soda, walked back to the car, and drove away. The trunk was filled with whatever the order was, and by 7 or 8 that evening, I would go to Ho Jo's on Route 128 or in the high school parking lot to distribute the booty. Thank god I never got stopped by the police.

Every weekend, I was getting everyone drunk at my high school. I made money from every transaction; it was my service fee. One of my yearbook entries said, "Hey Berman, thanks for the shit face shows!" Distributing liquor, beer, and wine, I was in more demand than I could have imagined. I had so many friends. It was wild. In my later years, I realized that it was my first business. It was also the beginning of my understanding of "networking." This became a precious skill that I still leverage to this day.

Having the Chrysler allowed me much freedom and got me into more mischief. I took the Rabbi's daughter, and we would skip out of Hebrew school; I would let her drive the car. I had her drive to the back of the temple, where privacy and seclusion existed. Don't ask! I also took my dates to the Babson campus to "show them the world."

- **Woodstock**

August 1969, Woodstock was an EPIC once-in-a-generation experience. It was an event that changed me forever. As my buddies and I stepped onto the sprawling fields of Max Yasgur's farm in Bethel, New York, crowds of fellow young people stretched as far as the eye could see - a sea of long hair, topless and naked, guys and girls, colorful clothes, and joyful faces all united by a shared love of music and a desire to come together in peace and harmony. The air was thick with the scent of incense, marijuana, and the earthy musk of so many bodies congregated closely together.

Legendary musicians took to the stage, their powerful voices and rousing melodies igniting euphoria in the massive crowd. We danced and swayed to the pulsing rhythms and revealed in the sublime magic of the live performances, our souls stirred by the artists' raw passion and talent. In between sets, I wandered the grounds, meeting friendly strangers from all walks of life. We shared food, conversation, and a profound sense of community and connection. It was free love!

I'll never forget when the sky got dark and the real fun began. The sky rained down on our party, and mud soon permeated the gathering. It did little to dampen spirits—we banded together, determined to revel in this once-in-a-lifetime experience no matter the conditions. Woodstock was more than just a concert; it was a cultural milestone, an affirmation of the power of music, love, and unity. It was an unforgettable moment of history that I knew would resonate throughout my lifetime.

Getty Images

As I navigated the twists and turns of my early adulthood, I faced a new challenge: the draft. The year was 1969, and the draft was in full swing. For far too many young Americans, a low number in the lottery meant one thing—you were bound for the jungles of Vietnam. It was a time of great uncertainty and unrest as the country grappled with a profoundly unpopular conflict, tearing it apart at the seams.

As luck would have it, I had a low draft number and no control over whether I would be shipped to the front lines in Vietnam. **(Refer to Mom and Hilda.) I opted to join the Reserves and spread my time over

seven years, guaranteed to be on stateside duty. I tested in advance and
was classified as a medic specializing in surgical nursing.

-The Army Reserves-

I was at a crossroads after moving to Detroit to pursue my
education. With the Vietnam War raging and the draft in full swing, I
knew my future was uncertain. Determined to serve my country while
continuing my studies, I enlisted in the Army Reserves.

Before I could begin my specialized training, I had to complete
boot camp at Fort Polk, Louisiana. To say I was not looking forward to
this experience would be an understatement. Fort Polk, which I called
the "Armpit of the Earth," was notorious for its harsh conditions and
grueling training regimen.

From the moment I arrived, reality hit me like a ton of bricks. The
intake process was a whirlwind of activity, starting with a complete
head shave to delouse all incoming recruits. As I watched my hair fall
to the ground and felt the unfamiliar lightness of my newly-shorn head,
I realized that my life was about to change in ways I could never have
imagined.

Next, I was issued my uniform, a tangible symbol of the
commitment I had made and the challenges that lay ahead. I felt pride
and trepidation as I donned the fatigues and boots, knowing I was now
part of something much larger than myself.

They included physical training, drills, and classroom instruction
in the following weeks. Louisiana's heat, humidity, and mosquitoes
made every day a test of endurance and resilience.

-Anecdotes: Grits and KP Duty

The first time I was in line for food was at breakfast, and the
sign outside described the menu. I'm a boy from the Northeast. I was
introduced to "hominy grits" for the first time; it's the comedian-wise
guy in me, and I said aloud, "How many of those grits can I have?" Well,
that was the wrong thing to say.

Within seconds, the drill sergeant pulled me out of the line and told me I would do KP for the next 24 hours. KP, what the heck! In 24 hours, there were six of us cracking eggs, sweating, and throwing eggshells into this giant industrial-sized mixing bowl. The same experience happened while peeling potatoes, throwing them into a machine, and sweating inside. I avoided the mess hall at all costs moving forward.

-Anecdote: The 10-Mile March and a Reprieve

Another experience was while on patrol and during the 10-mile forced march. I stumbled and could fake my way out of the march."The unexpected hospital stay provided a welcome respite, a brief vacation amidst the rigors of training."

One of my other memories is that I got off the base every night and called my first wife and my company's headquarters back in Detroit. Oh yeah, I met my first wife, Betty. We only lasted three years. She was a teacher, and I was a long-haired filmmaker who kept wild hours, smoked weed, and drank lots of wine. The Marriage was not destined to make it.

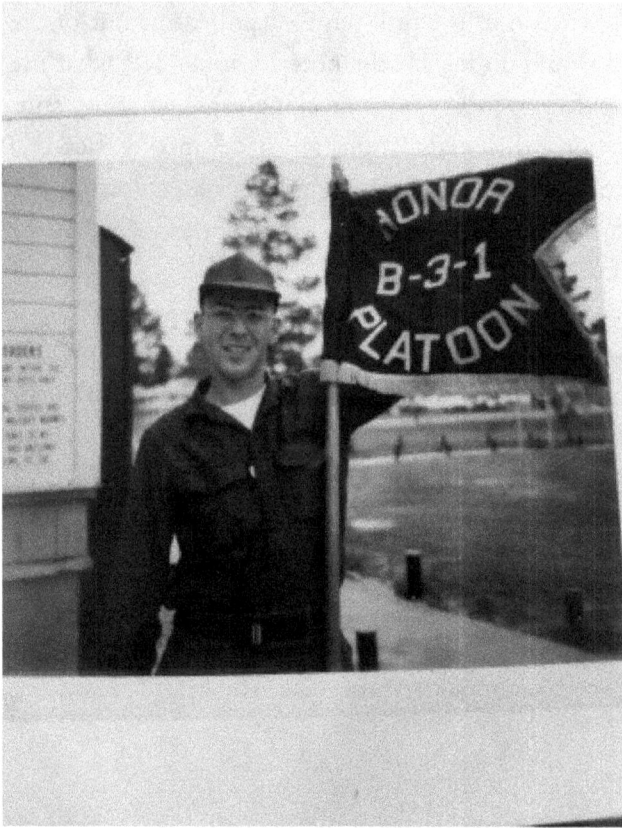

Navigating the Army Reserves

I would go on to serve my nurse training at FT Sam Houston, where I made friends with Tom Misch, whose dad was a bigwig at Ford Motor Company. He had a brand new, beautiful convertible Mustang, a fat wallet, and his uncle's estate, where we could hang out every night. We left campus at 4 PM and came back at 6 AM. We ate and drank well, and it made our time very bearable!

This was a stark difference from being in Louisiana. I had hands-on training to become a surgical nurse. The big takeaway and my own PTSD were from seeing a lot of guys my age come back from the front lines and caring for them. I considered attending school to become a nurse, but I wanted to stay involved in the creative side of the film business.

After my third year of service, I wore a short hair wig for two weeks to keep my hippie-style long hair a secret from my sergeants. When I returned home from a hot summer camp, I left Detroit and returned to Boston to finish serving in a more liberal political environment.

Despite the challenges of military life, I found solace in the camaraderie of my fellow soldiers. I forged great friendships, particularly with Tom Misch, whose family connections afforded us small luxuries and moments of fun amidst the rigors of training. Together, we learned the value of teamwork, perseverance, and finding joy in even the most difficult circumstances.

As my time in the Army Reserves ended, I realized that the lessons I had learned would stay with me forever. The discipline, adaptability, and resilience I had developed would serve as the foundation for my future entrepreneurial endeavors. I had learned to embrace challenges as opportunities for growth, to find humor in the face of adversity, and to rely on the support of others when needed.

My military experience was not just a detour but an essential part of my journey. It shaped me in ways I could never have anticipated and prepared me for the trials and triumphs ahead. As I moved forward, I carried with me the knowledge that no matter what obstacles I might face, I had the strength, skills, and determination to overcome them.

- Return to Boston

I returned to Boston, ready to embark on various careers. In the 1972/3-78 time frame, I created many opportunities. I met Peter Metrik, a long-haired, perpetually stoned guy who was getting into the cheesecake business. He asked for my help securing distribution at Star Market, which I gladly did. I had direct connections, so it was easy, and the cheesecake was NYC's finest, made at D'aiuto Bakery. As a thank you, he invited me to visit him in Jamaica, offering to cover my expenses. I jumped at the opportunity and found myself flying to Montego Bay, ready for an adventure.

-Anecdote: "Jamaica Man"!

Upon arrival, I had my first Red Stripe beer and a few puffs from a giant spliff that nearly knocked me out. As a young white guy in a third-world country, I felt strangely at home. The trip was magical, and I made friends with a Jamaican property owner in Negril. I convinced him to monetize his beachfront property by leasing it for a restaurant. I painted a picture of how it would benefit him and his family, and with a handshake, we had a deal.

Flying back to Boston, I told a friend about the opportunity; the rest was history. I brokered the deal. I found joy in procuring equipment and shipping it to the newly established Golden Sunset Restaurant on Negril Beach. Over the next year, I made frequent visits to Jamaica, and I facilitated the opening of a dive shop on the property.

I was getting paid handsomely, taking my compensation in the form of Jamaican weed, which I had transported back to Boston. This was a time before marijuana was legal, and although I did well financially during this period, I eventually stopped importing due to the risks involved.

Restaurant

bed   board   brew

Jamaican and Continental Cuisine

Welcome to the Golden Sunset Restaurant. We are proud to present to you a variety of fresh, local foods. Our menus vary from day to day, due to the supply available and our creative chef. He wants you to enjoy freshness and quality. We offer an expanding choice of freshly squeezed juices. Please inquire about the fresh baked pastries of the day, from Italian pannetone, Chocolate-rum cake and Sour sop custard to breakfast fruit breads.

Open for coffee - 8:30 a.m.

Continental Breakfast

orange or grapefruit juice,   bread,   jamaican coffee
3.00 Ja

Omlettes   and   Crepes

vegetable   cheese   ackee and saltfish   fruit crepe
4.00 Ja   5.00 Ja   5.00 Ja   4.00 Ja

Golden Sunrise
tia maria and orange juice
1.50 Ja

Buffet Brunch
monday - tuesday

juice, coffee, fruit bowl, plantain, pastry and chefs choice from the following selection of entrées:

lobster quiche, ackee and salt fish, eggs benedict, cheese pie and more.
6.00 Ja / person

-Scramble 1967-73

After returning to reality, I knew it was time to get serious about mapping out a career. I spent that summer working as a short-order cook at the Pancake Man on Route 28 and flipping burgers at Kemps, which became McDonald's in Hyannis. I had not emotionally dealt with my dad's passing. I was pretty numb! During this time of uncertainty and loss, I met Jack Penick, a fellow short-order cook who would become a close friend and mentor.

2. Motor City Dreams: Discovering My Passion for Film and Entrepreneurship

When Jack told me about a program that could get me into the prestigious University of Michigan campus in Ann Arbor, I knew I had to try it. The catch? First, I'd have to start at the Detroit campus and maintain a 3.0 GPA. I was up for the challenge. I moved to Detroit.

So, I packed my bags and headed to Michigan, ready to take on this new chapter. To support me, I landed a gig as a night bartender at "The Rat"—an authentic blue-collar joint frequented by auto workers. Let me tell you, being the first "Jewish guy" those guys had ever really interacted with was an eye-opening experience.

The real game-changer came when I signed up for a film studies course at Wayne State University. The campus was across the street from U of M. That's where I met Professor Roger Jackson, who invited me to work with his production company, Ultramedia. Talk about a dream come true! I jumped at the chance to be a "go-for" - a glorified gopher, if you will—and soak up as much knowledge as possible about the industry.

From sound and lighting to location shooting and editing, I dove in headfirst, eager to learn. And you know what they say - if you want something done right, do it yourself. So, I started positioning myself as an "executive producer and entrepreneur" of sorts, leveraging my sales skills to bring in new projects. It was a hustle, for sure, but the hands-on experience I was gaining was priceless.

Looking back, my decision to move to Detroit and immerse myself in that blue-collar, gritty environment was one of the best things I ever did. It challenged and stretched me and gave me a new appreciation for the value of hard work and perseverance.

So here I am, a long way from my initial collegiate aspirations, but loving every minute of the journey. Detroit may not have been on my radar at first, but it's where I found my footing, honed my skills, and set the stage for all the adventures to come. And you better believe I'm grateful for every step of the way.

- Anecdote: My First Professionally Produced Commercial

In the early 1970s, this was an exciting path for me. I created *opportunities* by calling the creative directors at advertising agencies and then producing the projects. It was the opportunity I was looking for. I liked the idea of working for myself. I admit to being addicted to the chase (sales), creating my projects and opportunities, and executing them. I was taking huge risks. Here is where I "built grit" and learned to "ride the roller coaster" without being too nauseous.

It all started when I met Jim Watring, the creative director at Stone and Simons, an ad agency. The two of us hit it off right away, and before long, we'd devised a plan to create a low-budget commercial for his client, United Shirt Distributors.

I would be the producer and handle all the behind-the-scenes stuff. My job was to set up the shoot, get the appropriate equipment, run the sound, and be the PA (Production Assistant). I recruited the Michigan State wrestling team to meet us in East Lansing at dawn. What is the incentive to get them to show up? A case of beer for each person, of course.

So there we were 18 brave souls braving the early morning chill as the sun started to rise. And let me tell you, the scene that unfolded was pure gold. We had hung an array of Shirts on the tree limbs. These burly wrestlers started yelling and beating their chests, running down the hill, all while a considerable speaker blasted funky, colorful music. We got that first shot of the sunrise just right, and then we went in for the close-ups, capturing the guys putting on their shirts and flashing those big muscles and happy grins.

The shoot took about two hours, and when we were done, we rewarded each wrestler with a case of beer. We won an ANDY, a local advertising award, acknowledging our effort.

-Anecdote: Sussman

I had an incredible learning experience when I went on a joint sales call with one of the best sales and promotion guys I had ever met - Alan Sussman, an advertising legend in Detroit. (The Sussman Agency) At the time, Alan was the director of Tallman Music, and I represented Ultra Media.

Alan had scheduled an appointment with Ron Advari, the creative director at the agency. Al Burton, the art director, and Dan Ellithorpe, the executive producer, were also in attendance. When we entered Ron's office, Alan did something unexpected - he lifted his leg, putting his vast leather cowboy boot right on Ron's immaculate expensive desk, and boldly proclaimed, "You will make the biggest mistake of your life if you don't hire the two most creative companies in Detroit."

I was shocked by Alan's audacious move, but that was just his style. Alan was a big, bold personality in the ad business. He knew how to command attention and sometimes get the company by being outrageous.

In the end, Alan's unconventional approach worked brilliantly. We were both able to get into the agency and land the deal that very day. It was a master class in the art of persuasion.

Working with Alan that day taught me so much about salesmanship, thinking on your feet, and having the confidence to take bold, decisive action. His larger-than-life presence and knack for the theatrical made a significant impression on me. That experience with an advertising giant like Alan was unforgettable and invaluable in shaping my career in the industry.

As I pursued my studies and honed my photography and film skills, I became increasingly drawn to entrepreneurship. I realized that my passions could be more than just creative outlets; they could be the foundation for a successful business venture.

Looking back on this pivotal chapter, I realize that the challenges and uncertainties I faced were essential to my growth as an artist and an entrepreneur. They taught me the importance of resilience, adaptability, and staying true to one's passions in facing challenges. But beyond the work ethic, Detroit taught me the power of relationships. The connections I made there, from my fellow factory workers to Professor Roger Jackson, would become the foundation of my entrepreneurial network. I learned that success is never a solo journey - it's constantly built on a web of relationships, each supporting and propelling you forward."

As my skills grew, so too did my responsibilities. I transitioned into the role of chief evangelist, marking my entry into the world of professional sales. My enthusiasm and drive proved valuable assets, and I soon produced projects for AAA and Filenes. It was a thrilling time, filled with long hours, hard work, and the satisfaction of seeing my efforts translate into tangible results.

3. Charley's and the Chestnut Hill Mall

While hustling for film work, I landed a gig as a bartender at Charley's Saloon at the Chestnut Hill Mall, working the night shift. It was a fantastic time; the mall was new, and the saloon was a huge hit. I met countless people (karma?) who would set me on various escapades.

Here are some memories from that time.

The Chestnut Hill Mall was buzzing with activity, a vibrant hub of commerce and social connection. Against this lively backdrop, I tended the bar at Charley's Saloon, a famous watering hole that attracted a diverse clientele. The vibrant atmosphere and constant hum of conversation provided the perfect stage for my nightly "behind-the-bar performances."

Working at Charley's Saloon and Zelda's taught me invaluable lessons about the power of networking, the importance of adaptability, and the art of building relationships. These skills would later prove crucial as I navigated the challenges of starting and growing my businesses.

With my outgoing personality and quick wit, I relished engaging with the patrons, striking up conversations, and pouring drinks with a flourish. The venue always attracted a vibrant and diverse clientele, reflecting the free-spirited social climate of the era. I immersed myself in the energy and camaraderie, forging connections with individuals from all walks of life.

In addition to my bartending duties at Charley's, I also worked the night shift at Zelda's, a local disco. There, I embraced my role as the "dancing bear," entertaining the crowd with my exuberant moves as I mixed cocktails. The experience honed my people skills and allowed me to cultivate a vast network of acquaintances - including many intrigued female patrons.

In late 1974, while still working at Charley's and producing a film, I was approached by a representative of the Sonnabend Group, a large hotel company in Boston. They were planning a bicentennial event in Washington, DC, and I was flattered when they asked me to be part of the team conducting a feasibility study and logistics assessment. I took the gig, even though it meant spending 3 to 4 days a week in DC and juggling my responsibilities. After two months, the project was abandoned, but it was still a prestigious feather in my cap.

Around the same time, during an afternoon shift at Charley's, I was approached by Alan Folsom, a writer and partner at the Abbey Group. They converted two movie theaters in Kenmore Square into a disco and invited me to become their general manager. I jumped at the chance and threw myself into setting up the place, hiring staff, and ordering top-shelf liquor. Having been around the restaurant and hospitality business, I quickly grew into the position.

During this time, also at Charlie's Salon, I met my wife Ellen, who worked at the mall. I was smitten, and not only did she become my GF/Fiance, but I also hired her as my head waitress. We had a blast, making tons of cash and living the high life. On our nights off, we dined at some of Boston's finest establishments, and the servers and bartenders reciprocated our generous tips. It was lucrative to be in the business, and we spent thousands partying like crazy all night. Working alongside Ellen was a turning point in my personal and professional life. Her support, encouragement, and partnership were invaluable as I navigated the challenges and triumphs of my early entrepreneurial ventures. Our shared experiences during this time laid the foundation for a bond that would carry us through the ups and downs of our journey together over 37 years."

As Mirage was a considerable success, 3,000 square feet of space was still available, so we opened KIX, a jazz club. We had early performances by Donna Summer, Brandon Marsailes, and Miles Davis. We also had our share of visits from Marvelous Marvin Hagler and other notable sports figures. It was a lot of fun, and we made a ton of money.!

4. The Call of Hollywood

From a young age, I was captivated by Hollywood's allure. My uncle Lloyd, a pioneering figure in 3D photography and adult film production, ignited a spark within me with his dashing good looks and incredible business savvy. His tales of chasing his dreams out West and striking gold fueled my entrepreneurial ambitions as I hung onto his every word, mesmerized by his magnetism and unwavering drive.

When my uncle would visit, he'd bring the latest cinematic equipment—Brownie and Polaroid cameras, 3D rigs, and other cutting-edge tools of the trade. These gifts and the stories of his exploits only deepened my fascination with the world of visual storytelling and the power of entrepreneurship.

As I navigated the dynamic landscape of the restaurant and nightlife industry, I found myself drawn to the thrill of the chase, the ability to create opportunities and bring visions to life. These experiences honed my adaptability, salesmanship, and knack for building meaningful connections - all of which would prove invaluable as I continued my entrepreneurial journey.

I hung on his every word, mesmerized by his tales of heading out West, chasing his dreams and striking gold. The way he commanded a room, the sheer magnetism he exuded - And I wanted nothing more than to follow in his entrepreneurial footsteps and carve out my path. Lights, cameras, action!

But as I reflect on my Hollywood dreams of the past, I can't help but feel a profound sense of gratitude. My uncle's infectious entrepreneurial spirit and unapologetic passion for visual storytelling set me on this course.

-Anecdotes: Lloyds Influence

As I reflect on my uncle Lloyd's life and influence, I can't help but feel a deep sense of comfort and solace. In many ways, he represented the embodiment of the life I had always imagined for my father before his untimely passing.

Remember, my dad died suddenly in Nantucket in July of '64, leaving a gaping hole in my life. But being around Lloyd, seeing how he navigated the world with such boundless energy and ambition, allowed me to fill in those missing pieces. In my mind's eye, I could fantasize and envision how my father's life might have further unfolded had he been given the chance to realize his dreams.

Lloyd's larger-than-life persona and his unwavering entrepreneurial spirit served as a proxy for the father I had lost. I found solace in watching him operate, bearing witness to the fulfillment he derived from his various business ventures and creative pursuits. I could channel my father's spirit through my uncle, allowing me to grieve the past while finding inspiration for the future.

Lloyd's enthusiasm for life and business was contagious. Through our conversations, whether out on the water or back on land, he shared invaluable lessons about the importance of taking risks, thinking big, and never giving up on your dreams. These insights would later become the foundation of my entrepreneurial philosophy.

With my dream coming to fruition with my feet planted in Hollywood, I scored a gig to produce a commercial set for Dunkin' Donuts with a young child actor named Mason Reese, a freckled, red-haired, smart kid. It was a great shoot. I worked for a Boston agency. The agency owner hit it off with my wife, and she told him she was homesick. I did not know he was a con man liar; he took advantage of Ellen's homesick information. The next day, he offered me a plum producer job in his agency. He painted a rosy picture; Ellen bought it hook, line, and sinker; there was no question she wanted to go back east.

Though my initial Hollywood venture may not have panned out as I had hoped, the experience only fueled my restless entrepreneurial spirit. The thrill of chasing my passions, the determination to overcome obstacles, and the unwavering belief in my abilities - these were the qualities that would continue to define my path, guiding me through the ups and downs of my remarkable entrepreneurial odyssey.

My Hollywood dream drifted away in the sunset for the sake of love

Once we arrived back in Boston, I was shocked to hear my offer had been reduced by 30%. So, even before I started, I had a terrible taste in my mouth. I made the best of it and produced a cooking show for Star Market called "Cooking with Kate McCarthy." This was successful, and I secured my position with the agency.

Part III

Formation of the Entrepreneurial Mindset

1. Sowing the Seeds of Success: My First Forays into Business

Now, with the agency shorting me. I was seeking some ways to generate additional income. Here is an example of me creating an opportunity with my thoughts!!! I was watching a news broadcast when I heard that John Carver, Director of the Massachusetts Council on Crime and Correction, would create an educational film to address prison recidivism. The following day, I got on the phone, called John, and made an appointment. I walked out with an agreement to produce a film with him.

My first documentary film was called "Petty John Report to the OIC (Officer in Charge)." Polaroid sponsored it, and I staged an interview with the President of Polaroid, who would go into the prison yard and talk about the programs needed to stop the revolving door. The film won 2nd place in the documentary category at the New York Film Festival.

This event marked the beginning of my journey as a documentary filmmaker. I poured my heart and soul into the project, determined to shed light on the critical issue of prison recidivism. Working with John and the Massachusetts Council on Crime and Correction was an eye-opening experience. I gained a deeper understanding of the challenges faced by prisoners and the criminal justice system.

Securing sponsorship from Polaroid was a significant milestone, as it provided the necessary resources to bring the project to life. I was thrilled to have the opportunity to stage an interview with a prisoner in the prison yard, giving them a platform to share their perspective on the programs needed to break the cycle of recidivism. How the hell did I do this? I picked up the phone and dialed the executive secretary gatekeeper, told her about the project, and soon after that, got a commitment to film at Norfolk prison.

The film's success at the New York Film Festival was a proud moment. Winning 2nd place in the documentary category validated my hard work and dedication to the project. It also catalyzed my growing passion for using film as a medium to explore critical social issues and inspire change.

This experience laid the foundation for my future work as a storyteller. It taught me the power of collaboration, the importance of giving voice to marginalized communities, and the potential for film to make a real difference.

As I continued navigating the challenges and opportunities of my entrepreneurial journey, I carried the lessons learned from this early success. It fueled my determination to keep pushing boundaries, seek out new ways to make an impact, and never stop believing in the power of a well-told story.

Little did I know then just how far this path would take me or how many more adventures and challenges lay ahead. But armed with the confidence and skills I had gained from this first foray into documentary filmmaking, I was ready to take on whatever came my way, one project at a time.

The exposure from my previous work opened the door to my next project: I created a fundraising film for the Eye Research Institute of the Retina Foundation. I wanted to make a real impact. I decided to focus on retinitis pigmentosa, an eye disease that can lead to blindness, and film four situations related to this condition; I strived to capture the participants' raw emotions and vulnerability throughout the filming. It was a delicate balance, but I felt fortunate to have gained their trust. They opened up to me, sharing their fears, hopes, and the daily struggles they faced living with this disease. I elicited a tear from a very stoic father of a boy losing sight.

When the film was complete, I was filled with pride and accomplishment. Not only had I created a powerful tool for raising awareness and funds for the Eye Research Institute, but I had also given a voice to those living with retinitis pigmentosa.

The hard work paid off when the film won the Houston Film Festival for Best Documentary. It was humbling to know that my passion for storytelling could make a real difference in people's lives.

Best of all, the film raised $750,000 for the foundation!

Looking back, I realize that this project taught me the importance of empathy and the power of capturing authentic emotions on film. These lessons have stayed with me, guiding me through future projects.

-Anecdotes: I came, I saw, I failed. The early Eighties

I had an agreement with a shoe manufacturer and distributor in PA to bring a new sneaker to the market. It was called **TVAS** (Toe ventilation air system), the shoes that could breathe. The company did not have exclusive distribution rights and did not have enough capital. They lied to me.

Peter Jeffer and I invented a **triple-edge windshield wiper** and a device to clean the blade. It never made it to market. We got a mold made and a small production run, but we could never get to the market. The space was undercapitalized, with many big players. Someone else came out with a similar product.

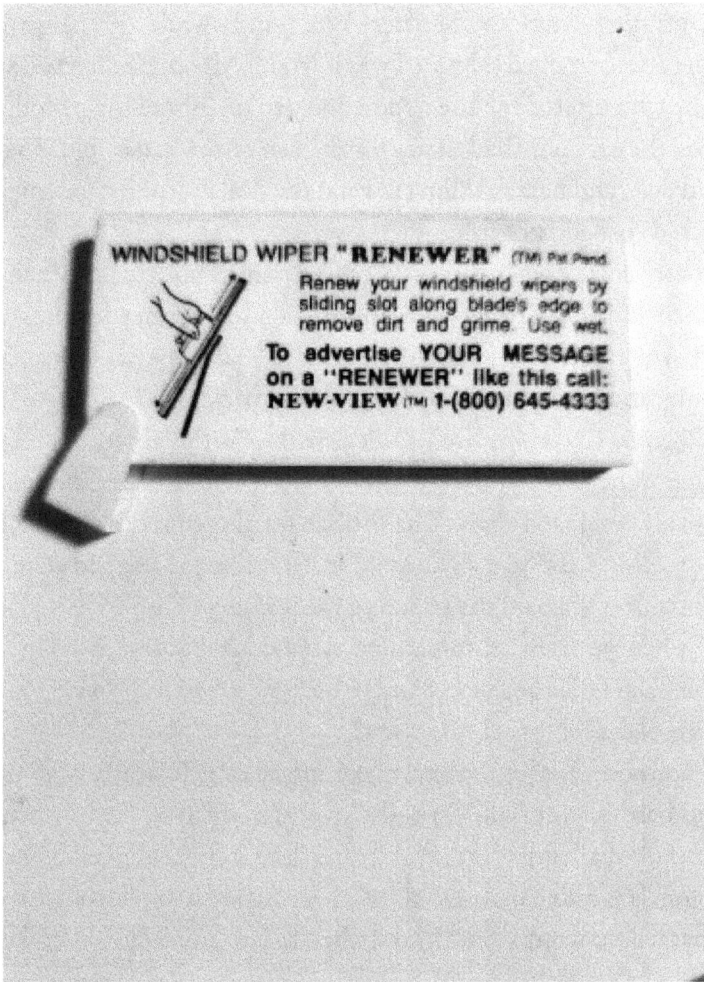

WINDSHIELD WIPER "**RENEWER**" (TM) Pat Pend.
Renew your windshield wipers by sliding slot along blade's edge to remove dirt and grime. Use wet.
To advertise YOUR MESSAGE on a "RENEWER" like this call:
NEW-VIEW (TM) **1-(800) 645-4333**

The following parody was **Flexi Floss,** a new rubber-derived gentle dental floss. It was the most comfortable flossing, and the thinnest rubber strips soothed your gums. However, we needed help figuring out how to consistently cut and package the rubbery substance. We found a machine costing us thousands of dollars upfront, so we decided to abandon the project.

   -Seattle: A Fish Story

During a trip to Seattle, WA, and while investigating a retort-packed smoked salmon, I was introduced to an Indian tribe elder (Dean) who offered me the opportunity to distribute their product in the Northeast. I only had to pay for the fish once I had it sold. That was a good deal, and he was willing to fund the deal except for the shipping. I ordered six pallets of fish.

It arrived at Logan Airport. I rented a small box truck. When I got to the airport, some pallets needed to be loaded. We needed the correct truck, which was lower than the dock. To make matters worse, it was freezing, and we had to offload 10,000 fish packages.

Oh, yes, I was surprised to deal with additional airport fees and drayage. When we got back to Sudbury a few hours later, we took the pallets and reloaded them. The fish sat for three months before I was able to sell it. I found a small store in Petersham, MA, and purchased the entire lot. We paid the tribe and made a small profit.

"When you fail at something, you don't become a failure as a person." You failed at a task. "And to become successful, you have to fail at many tasks."

I learned that it's OK to make mistakes. (To learn how not to be too hard on yourself.) In today's vocabulary, it's called Pivot! Fail! Test... fail! Fail fast. There is a fine line between persistence and delusion. (It's called insanity.) I have been lucky to develop a great sense of what will or won't work. Know when to bail and let go. "Know when to hold 'em." or When to throw 'em."

2. Fatherhood and Entrepreneurship: Navigating the Hero's Journey

From 1978 to 1993, I learned the value of persistence and mustered the courage to get my career started for real. We were pregnant, due Feb 7, with our first child, Jennifer, when we experienced The Blizzard of '78. It was a historic nor'easter that paralyzed the Northeast with massive snowfall and hurricane-force winds from February 5-7, 1978. Many areas saw over 2 feet of snow, with drifts reaching 15 feet high. Fierce winds created white-out conditions, making travel nearly impossible as people became stranded on highways and city streets for days. Fortunately, Jen waited until February 10th. We had a baby and a new third career/job," being a father.` `) Now, I had real responsibilities and had to feed more than me.

I want to share something profound that I learned about in the early 2000s - the hero's journey. Back then, raising a family based on a society that had some rigid expectations for men, especially white men like myself. We were supposed to be the breadwinners, the husbands, and the workers; we had to be the rock and foundation of our families. That's a lot of pressure, you know?

But it struck a chord when I started learning about the concept. It gave me a chance to step back and reflect on all those expectations that were placed on me as a white male during that time. I realized I wasn't alone in feeling the weight of those responsibilities.

The hero's journey is about the challenges and obstacles someone faces while striving toward a goal or a higher purpose. And man, did I feel that in my own life! Trying to be everything to everyone—the perfect husband, father, and provider—was sometimes exhausting.

But you know what? Reflecting on that hero's journey concept helped me **understand that having only some answers is OK. It's OK to stumble and face setbacks along the way.** The important thing is to keep pushing forward and learn and grow from those experiences.

Looking back, I'm grateful for the lessons I learned during that time. It wasn't always easy, but it shaped me into who I am today. And now, I have a deeper appreciation for the unique challenges and pressures of being a man in this society. *It's not about being perfect - it's about being authentic and doing your best with what you have.*

3. Fueling Innovation: The Rise and Fall of Greenwood Energy

During this time, I crossed paths with an entrepreneur named Mel Bowser. Mel was a larger-than-life character with an infectious personality that immediately drew me in. Looking back, I realize that we both recognized a mutual need in each other. I was captivated by the concept of this new technology. The idea of a stove that could heat an entire house without splitting green wood logs was revolutionary, especially for those who relied on wood for heating.

Mel entrusted me with the sales responsibility and hired an experienced tradesman to manufacture the stoves. It was a steep learning curve, and I quickly discovered the challenges of being a manufacturer without sufficient funding to produce enough stoves. The refractory materials required were also hard to come by, adding to our difficulties. A refractory oven or stove is designed to withstand extremely high temperatures. Through this experience, I learned valuable lessons: With adequate funding, marketing, and manufacturing are two distinct aspects of a business that only sometimes go hand in hand. It was a hard truth to face, but one that would serve me well in the future.

Despite the setbacks, working with Mel was an unforgettable adventure. His passion and drive were contagious, and even though the venture did not pan out as I had hoped, I walked away with a wealth of knowledge and a newfound respect for the intricacies of running a business.

I am grateful for the lessons learned and the memories made. It was a time of personal and professional growth, and it laid the foundation for the entrepreneur I would eventually become.

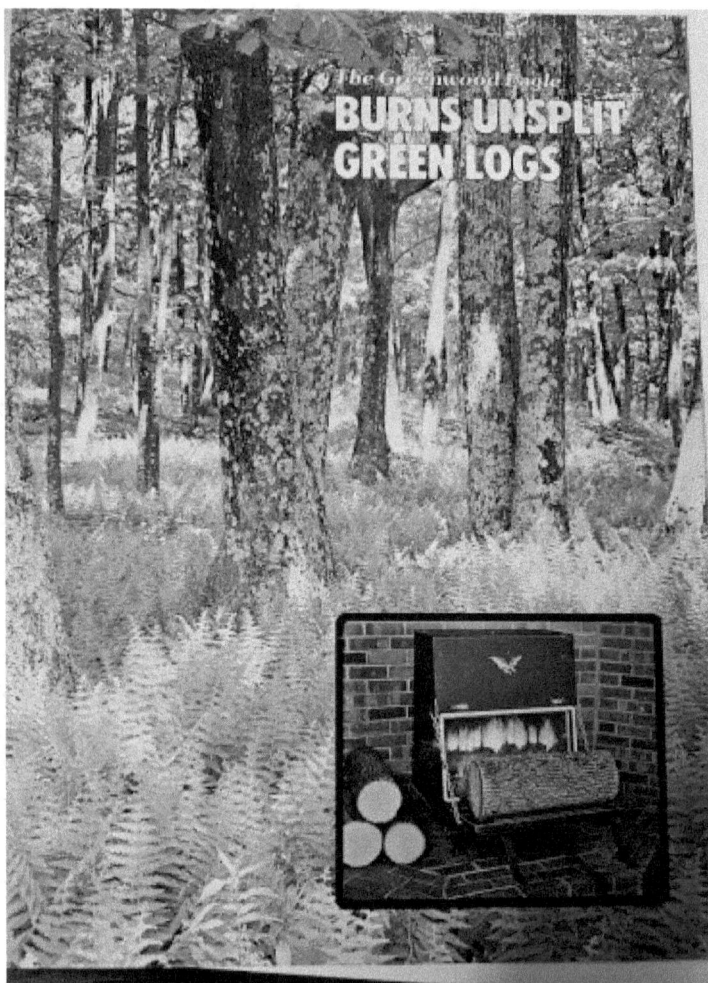

The Greenwood Eagle
BURNS UNSPLIT
GREEN LOGS

4. Juggling Family and Fortune: The Challenges of Being a Young Entrepreneur

I learned about the constant need for apple juice and diapers! I hustled a job as a producer and rep for a music producer, Tallman Music, and Stan Lang Productions. Stan's claim to fame was the famous commercial for Hertz, where they dropped a guy in the driver's seat of a convertible on Madison Avenue. A fantastic feat for the time, it put Stan on the map, so it was easy to open the doors at the agencies. I had immediate success, sold the Monday Night Baseball theme to ESPN, and produced commercials for advertising agencies J Walter Thompson and Wells Rich & Green (The NYC hustle was much like the TV series Mad Men).

As luck and fate might have it, Right at the time of hitting my stride, my wife's dad passed, and we moved back to Boston. I needed a new gig!

I never stopped being enamored with being an entrepreneur and building something that might someday be a company someone else values and desires to own. I'm in my early 30s and still remember what my mother said. *Dream big, and maybe your dreams will come true one day.*

Part IV

Ignoring Risk

My first start-ups taught me a lot because I ignored risk *(because I didn't know what risk was)* and plunged in because I wanted to start my own business and needed to support my family. Stephanie, my second daughter, was born in 1981 while we were back in Boston.

To support my family and my dreams of becoming a filmmaker, I freelanced and obtained a license to sell health insurance. It was a job I detested, constantly seeking employment or a project in the expanding computer industry. During this time, I also represented a magician from Worcester named Steve Daquiri, who was quite a character. I quickly realized the reality of supporting a growing middle-class family and making movies was fun and fabulous if you were single. So, I had to put the filmmaker's dream part of my life on hold.

- Steve Daquiri Magic

Working with Steve was a constant riot. I secured him a gig on a cruise ship and even negotiated with Caesars Palace to get him his room to perform. Steve was a highly accomplished close-up magician, and it was a privilege to witness his close-up magic behind the scenes firsthand.

During this time, Steve and I also produced a humorous live show featuring an Italian-Jewish wedding. We performed in Natick and Boston at various hotels. I made the show, and Steve directed it. For me, I was known as the father of the bride's gynecologist, Dr. Goldfinger. I got my degree at the "Y" and many more edgy lines. The show had a two-year run on Fridays and Saturdays.

Although I was slightly burned out, each weekend brought in much-needed dollars. I had 50% of the gate taken, a significant amount of money then. It helped me keep my dreams alive while providing for my family.

Looking back, I realize that this period of my life was a testament to my resilience and determination.

Even though I was stuck in the insurance business, which I hated, I found ways to pursue my creative outlet and passion for entertainment and creative expression. The experience with Steve and the live wedding show taught me the importance of networking, negotiations, and the power of laughter.

1. Pivoting with Purpose: Embracing Change and Opportunity

While selling insurance, I met Gerry Greenstein, who offered me the opportunity to partner with him. A millionaire from Rhode Island had funded him. He provided me with a consistent paycheck, a new car, and some sense of security—and partnership—I was a partner!

As I began to navigate this new landscape, I quickly realized that the path to success took a lot of work. Together, we launched International Techware, a consulting and lead generation company focused on cutting-edge technologies. We offered telemarketing research, outbound calling, "dialing for dollars," and customer prospecting.

- Access Technologies

Our first client was Access Technologies, a Software Developer (Pre-Lotus 123) with an "electronic spreadsheet" for all the big mainframes from Digital Equipment in Maynard, MA. I got my bug or love for introducing new technologies and being a part of the pieces or guts it took to make a start-up work, to get on the "chessboard." (One of my early heroes was Alan Klutchman, the founder of Access). I could see my future, which reminds me of the line from The Graduate where Dustin Hoffman gets advice to go into plastics, as that was the future. Mine was "Computers".

I did not know about computers or spreadsheets when I started my journey in the digital world. The earliest version of the desktop computer I used was a Data General machine with a huge green TV tube screen. I also became familiar with Wang and Digital "mainframes" advanced machines that paved the way for the technology we have today. We relied on lists and telephone numbers to complete our work in those days.

I began dialing for dollars, cold-calling CFOs, and asking them how they handled their spreadsheet work and analysis. The tools of the trade back then were paper and a calculator. I would inquire about the most significant purchases they made for millions of dollars and tell them about the electronic spreadsheet.

My success was due to tenacity, creativity, and the ability to communicate effectively with potential clients. I knew how to understand their needs and present a solution that could revolutionize their work processes.

- Mastering the Art of "Dialing for Dollars"

In the 1980s, when landlines and printed directories were still the norm, the ability to effectively "dial for dollars" was a critical skill for entrepreneurs like myself. Unlike today's landscape, where cold calls are often met with automated responses or immediate rejection, back then, people answered their phones - a concept that now seems almost quaint.

I reveled in the challenge of honing my craft as an executive telemarketer, pushing myself to connect meaningfully with potential clients. I learned I only wanted to speak to the decision-maker as early in my process as possible. I learned how to overcome the "Nos" in most sales processes. During this time, I found an unlikely ally in a brilliant numbers guy named Joel Berman (no relation). Joel took me under his wing, sharing invaluable insights that would transform my lead-generation efforts.

Joel taught me the key to breaking down my daily call activities into a simple, data-driven formula. For every 20 prospect calls I made, I could expect to generate four quality suspect leads, ultimately closing two deals. It was a revelation—a near-surefire system that felt almost like "printing money," as I liked to say. The 80/20 rule in action, with predictable results, never ceased to amaze me.

This experience taught me the mechanics of effectual cold calling and the power of leveraging data to drive business growth. I was a beast. I generated consistent opportunities by approaching lead generation with a systematic, analytical mindset, even in the face of rejection or uncertainty. This foundational skill would serve me well throughout my entrepreneurial journey.

The Lemon

Our next project was consulting for an EDP (Electric Protection Devices) start-up. We provided two major components for this business. We designed a production and assembly line to produce surge protection devices. Made in the USA, I created an advertising and media campaign, naming the device "The Lemon" (colored as a bright lemon), with the Tagline "The Lemon Sours Surges." We sold thousands of units to Computerland, one of the day's first chain retail computer establishments! We created the subsequent branding and advertising and purchased all the media. This event is the beginning of the computer business. I got the bug and went to the Giant Comdex show in Las Vegas. We extended the line with products called the Lime, Peach, and Grizzly (a backup battery). We innovated with a Lloyds of London Insurance policy to cover any computer attached to our devices. The cost was $1. The owner had enough cash to install a swimming pool in his backyard.

I didn't know that Jerry would provide me with many genius ideas, new projects, distractions, and chaos that coexisted with his manic-depressive disorder, a mental health condition. I was already working, and He was paying me and in manic mode." I was learning on the fly how to manage and deal with Gerry's vacillating mood swings. Trying to make sense of this was challenging, but I learned how to navigate his genius and craziness, and I believed I was in control. As I would find out, I wasn't.

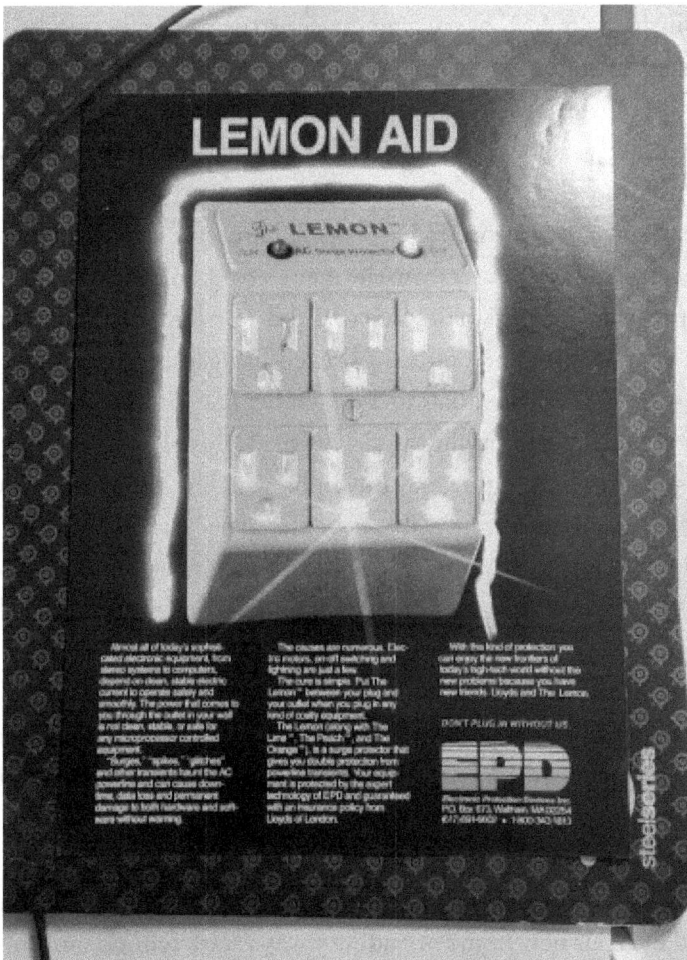

With the investor's money, Gerry created two development projects: an Executive home in Wellesley, MA, and a 96-unit condo project in Saugus, MA. I quickly learned that building an investment property was like producing and directing a movie. I had the right amount of peeps for the correct times in place. I had to become a logistics director, similar to directing a movie!

-Saugus- *"Timing is Everything"*

I was fortunate to purchase our first house in Northborough, Massachusetts. Saugus became my daily commute. I was up at 4 AM and on-site by 5 AM, overseeing the construction of 96 two-bedroom condos. I trusted my instincts. Real Estate Development was just like making a movie. Get organized!

The land was raw, and during the project's first days, the investor informed me that he had received a notice to cease. As the new property owners, we needed a proper "curb cut" (permission to cut open a curb for a driveway from the main road.), and the building could only proceed once it was rectified. I did not know it then, but this was a fatal blow to the project. I started navigating the town and the legalese to remedy the situation. I remember one meeting where we had a "consultant" in the city in the landowner's plush lawyer's office. Peter D was an imposing figure and the alpha male in the room. He let me know he had his handgun visible as he stated he "ran the town" and was the boss. We eventually got the curb cut, but it was six months later.

Once we could start, I faced numerous construction and design issues that cost time and money. Finally, we had the first units ready and the furnished model. We sold 67 units almost right away. Then, the crash of 2008 happened. The units weren't selling, and the vendors demanded payment. I had to navigate the bankruptcy court and so much more.

-Anecdote: Caught in the FBI's Crosshairs:

The unexpected visit from the FBI a few months after we had settled into our new home in Sudbury was a stark reminder of the need for transparency and diligence, even in the smallest of transactions. As I invited the agents inside, they explained they were there to inquire about a curious entry in the Saugus project's books - a line item marked simply as "bribe." I was baffled when I found out. I never got to ask her why she made the entry that way.

While the payment in question was not some clandestine pot of gold but rather a necessary step to expedite the approvals we required due to the significant delays we were facing, the mere mention of a "bribe" had triggered an investigation. Fortunately, I was not personally implicated, and the building inspector ultimately faced the consequences.

This unsettling incident underscored the importance of meticulous record-keeping and the need to navigate even the most innocuous-seeming transactions with the utmost care. As an entrepreneur, it's crucial to maintain the highest standards of integrity, ensuring that every action and decision can withstand the scrutiny of outside parties. This valuable lesson will serve me well in the years to come.

I was out of a job. For the next six months, I stood with the Magistrate on behalf of our investor, as his signature as guarantor was on everything. I faced angry tradespeople who were my buddies a few days earlier; now, they were sitting in front of a bankruptcy magistrate.

Throughout my life, I've always been one to take chances, embracing the philosophy that you miss 100% of the shots you don't take. This mindset has led me down many paths, some successful and others not. I've come, seen, and failed, but each failure has taught me valuable lessons and shaped me into who I am today.

While not every venture has been a triumph, the actual failure lies in not trying at all. So, I continue to take risks, knowing that even if I don't always succeed, I'm still growing, learning, and living life to the fullest.

2. The Birth of MB Enterprises

While the Saugus project fell off the cliff, I secured a property in Hudson, MA, where I built 18 industrial condominiums. I made enough from the project to sustain me for a while. I started networking and sold my success story about bringing EPD to market. I met a young Chinese entrepreneur, Kin Q, who had designed and built a "parallel processor," one of the first of its kind.

- The 1st Hard Drive subsystem for computer storage

I had yet to learn what this was. I quickly realized that this kind of software development was a very long and risky venture; during the build, Kin also discovered a technology breakthrough that led to the building of the first hard drive storage subsystem (a storage device attached to free-standing computers). This led to the importation of computer motherboards and their assembly in Massachusetts.

MB Enterprises contracted with Dragon Systems and created a marketing campaign for the Hard Drives, yielding over 30,000 "bingo card responses." Oh, my word, my office in Hopkinton was filled with postal bags. I was overwhelmed, got many pats on the back, and celebrated by leasing a 525i BMW. I believed we were on the way to making a fortune. I was WRONG!

The product worked perfectly on the" bench test" before being put into the shipping box, but when the equipment appeared on the customer's doorstep, it did not work. Why was this?

-Anecdote: The UPS Drop Test Challenge:

This is where I discovered the hard truth about passing a UPS drop test. The solution was easy. Invest in better packaging. Each custom box, with custom foam inserts, would cost $48 per box. There was a 12-week delay in getting the packaging. I saw how indecision led to failure. At the time, Kin decided not to invest in the boxes, abandoning the idea as he saw a much bigger opportunity. He lost his focus on chasing what was hot. The company needed help to deliver or execute the promise. The 30K leads generated were squandered.

Definition: UPS Drop Test: "A package drop test is a simulation of the falls that a package holding goods may experience during shipping and handling." In a controlled environment, a complete package (typically a carton with the correct item(s) inside) will be dropped in various ways (on corners, edges, and faces, in a particular order) to find any weaknesses or stress points that can then be addressed.

-Lesson: What the heck is a Motherboard?

Shortly after getting the BMW, Kin met me in the office. "Michael, I have good news and bad news. I said, "Bad." "Give Me the bad." Bad news: we are going out of business." OK, what's the good news? "Good News, We are starting a new business and building computers." He showed me 25 motherboards from Taiwan. The new company was AT Systems. We were going to private label custom computers.

-Anecdote: A Chance Encounter with Michael Dell

I stumbled upon a lucrative opportunity - we were advertising the availability of computer motherboards, and I was put in charge of managing those sales. Little did I know, this would be the spark that would ignite a meteoric rise.

One fateful afternoon, I received a call from a young go-getter named Michael Dell. To my delight, he ordered 12 of those precious motherboards. A few weeks later, he returned, requesting 50 more. I couldn't believe my luck - this was undoubtedly the start of a rocket ride to riches.

Or so I thought. I soon learned that building trust and nurturing relationships in the cutthroat world of technology sales was challenging, mainly because everything was conducted remotely over the phone or in hastily arranged face-to-face meetings. The landscape was ever-shifting, and the competition was fierce.

It wasn't long before I discovered that Michael had a few tricks up his sleeve. Leveraging his connections and resources, he could source those same motherboards at a much lower cost, cutting out the middleman - me. Of course, we had no formal agreement, so all was fair game in this high-stakes advertising war.

"I provided Michael with the first 62 motherboards" as the foundation for his burgeoning computer empire.

I was in denial and ignored the risk. Even though Kin abandoned the hard drive project, I still had the BMW and a family to feed. I went out on my own, became the representative of a system, and found that many businesses needed machines built just for them. There, I created sales opportunities and successfully hit the road to get custom computers, which were suddenly in significant demand.

3. The High Price of Trust: Learning from My Mistakes

I gained much knowledge about niche markets and in-person "consultative selling." I discovered the crucial factors to consider when deciding who should be present. I found a large number of customers who were interested in our company's products. I only dealt with the decision-maker. This served me well here and still does today, as I can enter any door I want! I only sell from the top down. Otherwise, your chance of closing diminishes by over 60 %. Why waste your valuable time?

More lessons learned and takeaways: Trust (read Steven Covey's "The Speed of Trust") and risk analysis.

It didn't take too long. I was anxious about not getting my commission checks on time. I had eight checks I was asked to hold as the cash flow was challenging. Kin promised I could cash the checks at the end of December. When I went to the bank to cash them, they were not honored. They gave me bad checks. This is a crime in the state of Massachusetts.

In the end, recovering took a lot of work, and I only managed to recoup a small portion of what I was owed. This experience taught me a valuable lesson that I will carry into future endeavors: it's crucial to incorporate a risk assessment component into my decision-making process when considering involvement in any project. The lawsuit pursuit proved to be financially draining and emotionally taxing, taking a significant toll on my family and personal relationships. It forced me to stop and reflect on the actual cost of such actions. In most situations, the effort and resources required to pursue legal action aren't worth it. The most effective safeguard is having a well-drafted written agreement from the outset. A solid contract can be filed away and may never need to be referenced again. However, if something goes wrong, having a written agreement to fall back on can make all the difference. It's always better to be proactive and have a clear understanding between parties in advance to mitigate potential risks and conflicts down the line.

My experience with Kin Q and Dragon Systems taught me many valuable lessons about the importance of thoroughly assessing a company's capabilities and capacity before committing to deliver a product or service. While I was excited about the potential of the new technology and the opportunity to promote it, I needed to recognize the company's limitations in executing the delivery of the product.

Looking back, I should have taken a more critical approach in evaluating Dragon Systems' ability to handle the overwhelming response generated by our marketing efforts. Had I done so, I could have foreseen the potential challenges in fulfilling the orders and worked with the company to develop a more realistic strategy for meeting customer demand. I was also desperate as I needed to stay afloat...even though I knew I had been disappointed by relying on Kin and his performance, I still went forward. I did not listen to myself!!! Note to self: *I needed to learn to think critically, do more risk assessments moving forward, and listen to my gut!*

This experience underscored *the importance of due diligence when partnering* with or promoting another company. It's crucial to assess a product or service's market potential and the company's infrastructure, resources, and processes to ensure they can deliver on their promises. By taking a more comprehensive approach to evaluating a company's capabilities, entrepreneurs can make more informed decisions and mitigate the risk of disappointing customers and damaging their reputations.

4. Thinking Outside the Box: Developing a Problem-Solving Mindset

Throughout my entrepreneurial journey, I've encountered numerous situations where I faced seemingly insurmountable challenges. However, one of the most valuable lessons I've learned is that even in the bleakest circumstances, there is always a solution if you remain resourceful and open to new approaches.

My experience with private-label computers is a prime example of this. When I found myself in a situation where I was making my decisions based on my desperation and neediness, I had no answers to a problem that desperately needed one. I still needed to provide my family with food and shelter. I could have easily given up and accepted defeat. However, I viewed the challenge as an opportunity to think creatively and explore alternative solutions.

I could immediately "pivot" so I "could think" I had a path to financial survival. By tapping into my network, leveraging my skills, and thinking outside the box, I could navigate the private-label computer market and find a path forward. I focused on healthcare providers as my Niche. This experience taught me that success often lies in our ability to adapt, pivot, and find unconventional ways to overcome obstacles. This only lasted briefly as well-funded companies such as IBM and other players came to the market with off-the-shelf boxes, and computers became mainstream.

As entrepreneurs, we must cultivate a mindset of resourcefulness and resilience. By embracing challenges as opportunities for growth and learning, we can develop the skills and confidence needed to tackle even the most daunting problems. This lesson has served me well throughout my career, reminding me that with perseverance and ingenuity, there is always a way to turn adversity into an advantage. **Note to Self:** Always consult a lawyer. The investment is worth it.

5. Under Pressure: Navigating the Stresses of Entrepreneurship

Man, being an entrepreneur in my early 30's was no joke. The pressure was intense, and it took a toll on my health. My blood pressure was through the roof, and I was packing on the pounds from all the stress eating and lack of exercise. I had mouths to feed - my kids who meant the world to me, a fancy BMW to pay off, rent to cover to keep a roof over our heads. Trying to juggle all that while pouring everything I had into my business, it's no wonder I was feeling the strain.

There were times when the stress got so bad I thought I might crack. I'd be up at all hours, mind racing a mile a minute trying to figure out how to overcome the latest crisis or cash flow crunch. It felt like I was being pulled in a hundred directions at once, with barely a moment to catch my breath. But somehow, I always found a way to push through. I've adopted this unshakable belief that there's always a solution, a way forward, even in the darkest times.

So, I'd dig deep, get creative, and do whatever it took to keep things afloat for my family and my dreams. Cut costs, chase down new leads, sweet talk creditors to extend payment terms. It was never easy, but I always told myself if I could just hang on and work the problem, I'd find a way through to the other side. And you know what? Somehow, I always did. I couldn't tell you how; maybe it was grit, luck, or providence, but I'd find that missing puzzle piece that made it all click into place. But man, I'm telling you the stress of it all - it was enough to make anyone go gray before their time. Not a road for the faint of heart, that's for damn sure.

Part V

Building a Legacy

1. From Startup to Success Story: The Incredible Journey of IDP

Standing at the crossroads of my entrepreneurial journey, I yearned for something more. The lessons I had learned and the experiences I had gained in my early career had prepared me for this moment, and I knew that the time had come to take a leap of faith and build something of my own.

In early 1993, I met Jim Walckner at a networking event. We couldn't have been more opposite in personality. We had many complementary skills. We recognized this as an opportunity to leverage our skill sets and started the IDP (Intelligent Document Processing), a document management integration and service provider. We had envisioned a paperless business. I was the chief evangelist and co-founder. We were a full-service provider of electronic document management business solutions.

I formerly served as the "Chief Marketing Officer," focusing on processing physical paper and re-engineering business practices and processes. I acquired our software, which became the cornerstone of the company's growth. I led the company into vertical markets, including retail hospitality, government nonprofits, banking, insurance, financial services, services, and transportation.

Pioneering New Technology

I pioneered ICR and OCR technologies (Intelligent and Optical Character Recognition) and helped revolutionize and streamline these services while integrating data processing systems. This is where I learned to be a" Business Process Engineer." I consulted with clients to change the paper process by leveraging cutting-edge digital technology. It was an easy sale that just made financial sense. I would have to recommend that the tech could displace 10 or 12 employees, and the savings were a no-brainer, as the payback fell in less than 18 months.

The following ten years were nothing short of amazing. Through sheer determination and grit, we managed to do the impossible, navigating the challenges of adequately financing the company. Our perseverance paid off when we met an incredible business owner in Sudbury, Massachusetts, who shared our vision.

Ted Pasquerrla, the visionary entrepreneur who owned a large business park, saw the immense potential in IDP. He took a chance on us, loaning us a $250,000 convertible note and building out our office space. We later paid back the $250 without giving up any equity. He had genuinely fallen in love with our business.

By the end of that remarkable 10-year stretch, we had generated significant revenue and grown our team to 38 dedicated employees. We were doing an impressive $14 million in sales—not bad! To accommodate our expansion, we had secured over 10,000 square feet of space from Ted!

-Anecdotes: Guerilla Marketing

To grow the company, we used "Guerrilla Marketing" (an unconventional, creative, and low-cost marketing strategy that aims to capture the attention of a large audience) to create a newsletter called "Image a Nation." We wrote stories and case studies about the efficacy of document management systems and promoted our services. We printed and mailed 5,000 copies to our acquired mailing list. Remember, there were no sophisticated marketing software programs to reach prospects; at least in the early 1990s, the internet was just being invented.

We reached broad business targets and generated many inquiries, which led us in many different directions. I began focusing on digital record-keeping for behavioral health and medical practices.

We developed a sister product to Infotrieve called MediTrieve for easy, secure access to medical records. I needed help reaching the direct decision-makers and hospitals in the Northeast region

One of my customers put me in touch with the Greater New York Hospital Association, and we made a solid case for them and got their support. It was a great tool to create credibility for us and the technology. They contacted the IT directors through their monthly newsletter and told them about this valuable technology. This became a huge revenue stream for the company.

-State Business

We were seeking business with the State of Massachusetts. I discovered that the process qualifications to get on a bidder's list were time-consuming and overwhelming. Instead, we established a relationship with an already-approved vendor and began bidding on their coattails; when we were successful, this was the start of our government services division.

The early days of IDP were marked by long hours, hard work, and a constant stream of challenges. We were pioneers in an emerging industry and knew that success would take time. But we were determined to succeed and poured our hearts and souls into building a company that would stand the test of time.

-Making Payroll

One particularly memorable challenge came when we faced the daunting task of meeting payroll for our growing team. We had 27 employees and their families counting on us, so I knew failure was not an option. As the clock ticked down and our bank account dwindled, I scrambled to find a solution.

In a moment of desperation, I reached out to our partner from the state, hoping against hope that he would be able to help us. To my surprise and relief, he agreed to advance us the funds we needed to cover payroll. I'll never forget the feeling of driving to his office in Waltham, picking up the check, and racing to the bank to deposit it before the 3 PM deadline. It was a close call, but we made it, and I learned the importance of building solid relationships and being resourceful in the face of adversity.

Another key lesson I learned during this period was the power of innovation and adaptability. We knew that to succeed in the rapidly evolving world of technology, we would need to stay ahead of the curve and anticipate the needs of our clients. And so, we invested heavily in research and development, constantly seeking new and better ways to serve our customers.

As IDP grew and evolved, so did my role within the company. I wore many hats, from sales and marketing to operations and finance. It was challenging and rewarding as I stretched myself beyond my comfort zone and learned to lead by example

2. Decade of Growth: Takeaways from My Time at IDP

Building IDP was not just a business venture but a labor of love. It was a testament to the power of hard work, determination, and unwavering belief in oneself.

But I also know our success was not due to my efforts alone. It resulted from a dedicated and talented team with unique skills and perspectives. It resulted from the support and encouragement of our families and loved ones, who stood by us through the highs and lows of our entrepreneurial journey.

Reflecting on my decade-long journey with IDP, I realize that my lessons have been invaluable in shaping my approach to entrepreneurship. One of the most crucial insights I gained was the importance of maintaining a diverse sales pipeline. By constantly seeking out new opportunities and nurturing relationships with potential clients, we were able to weather the ups and downs of the business world and ensure a steady flow of revenue.

"I saw the critical importance of this firsthand at IDP when we were faced with a significant cash flow crisis early on. By leveraging our diverse pipeline and securing a timely infusion of capital, we were able to weather the storm and emerge stronger. This experience taught me to prioritize building a robust sales funnel and maintaining a healthy capital cushion, and the lessons have served me well in all my subsequent ventures."

The most important lesson I learned at IDP was that **execution is everything.** Having a great idea or product is only half the battle; the ability to bring that vision to life separates successful entrepreneurs from the rest. This means relentless pursuit of excellence, paying attention to every detail, and striving to exceed expectations for every customer.

I see how these lessons have shaped my approach to entrepreneurship and guided me through the challenges and triumphs of my journey. By sharing these insights, I hope to inspire and empower others embarking on their entrepreneurial paths and provide a roadmap for success based on the real world, embracing adversity as a catalyst for growth. I've learned to view even the darkest circumstances through a lens of possibility. The setbacks were not punishments but lessons—painful, perhaps, but ultimately fortifying. They forced me to cultivate an adaptable mindset, become a creative problem-solver, and never take success for granted," add: "Looking back on my decade at IDP, I see how much those themes of resilience, adaptability, and relationships defined our success. We weathered countless storms, from financial crises to market shifts, always finding a way to bounce back stronger. We adapted to new technologies and customer needs, staying one step ahead of the curve. And we built a culture of collaboration and trust, knowing that our strength lay in our collective wisdom and effort. Those lessons would become the bedrock of my entrepreneurial philosophy going forward.

Note to self: I have reached two goals: providing jobs for people and earning over $14 million in sales revenue. We built a company that had value across the board.

I decided to leave and cash out of IDP. The company had reached about 14 million dollars in sales. As the tech revolution happened, I wanted to explore other emerging opportunities, and Jim wanted to remain focused. So I clocked out and went on my own to the next journey.

It took me about 18 months to figure out what to do next. I signed up for various short-term consulting projects.

-Navigating the Technological Revolution

As the 20th century drew close, the world was on the cusp of a technological revolution. The internet transformed how we lived, worked, and communicated, and the business landscape rapidly evolved. It was an exciting time to be an entrepreneur, and I knew I wanted to be at the forefront of this new frontier.

Fresh off the success of IDP, I found myself eager to explore new opportunities and challenges. The lessons I had learned about innovation, adaptability, and the power of hard work had prepared me for this moment, and I was ready to take on the world.

I knew the world of technology was not for the faint of heart. The dot-com boom was in full swing, and everywhere I looked, new startups were popping up, each promising to be the next big thing. It was a time of great opportunity and risk, and I knew I would need to be strategic in my approach.

The world was on the cusp of a technological revolution that would transform every facet of our lives - including how we do business. Looking back, I see how dramatically the rapid pace of innovation would challenge traditional entrepreneurial mindsets and models.

When I first started, the business landscape was vastly different. Sure, we had computers and some rudimentary telecommunications, but the speed at which new technologies emerged and consumer behaviors shifted differed from what I would encounter in the coming decades. It was a new ballgame, and I knew I would have to adapt my approach to stay ahead of the curve.

Gone were the days of relying solely on personal connections and face-to-face interactions to drive sales and growth. Suddenly, I had to navigate a complex digital ecosystem, learning the ins and outs of online marketing, social media, and e-commerce platforms. It was sink or swim, and I'll admit there were times when I felt utterly overwhelmed by the pace of change.

But I'm nothing if not resilient, and I was determined not to let technology leave me in the dust. I immersed myself in learning, constantly seeking new tools and strategies to understand better and engage with my customers. It wasn't easy—there were plenty of misfires and false starts. But with each new challenge, I grew more robust, adaptable, and innovative.

It wasn't just about staying ahead of the technology curve; I also had to grapple with the profound social implications of this digital revolution. The way people communicated, consumed information, and made purchasing decisions was shifting at a dizzying pace. I had to find ways to keep up, anticipate, and shape those evolving behaviors.

It was a delicate balance, to be sure. On the one hand, I wanted to leverage the power of technology to expand my reach, streamline operations, and deliver better experiences for my customers. On the other hand, I knew I couldn't lose sight of the human element - the importance of fostering genuine connections, building trust, and creating value beyond the latest digital bells and whistles.

Ultimately, navigating that technological landscape was one of the most significant tests of my entrepreneurial mettle. It required a level of agility, forward-thinking, and people-centricity that I had never before encountered. But you know what they say—**what doesn't kill you makes you stronger.** And I can say with certainty that the lessons I learned during that time have become the bedrock upon which all of my subsequent ventures have been built.

One of the critical lessons I learned during this period was the importance of staying true to my core values and vision. With so many new players entering the market and so much hype and noise surrounding the industry, it was easy to get caught up in the frenzy and lose sight of what truly mattered.

I also began to think more deeply about my purpose and legacy during this time. I had always been driven by a desire to impact the world positively, but now, I feel a renewed sense of urgency and responsibility to use my skills and resources for good.

As I looked to the future, I knew I wanted to focus on projects and ventures that generated profits and made a meaningful difference in people's lives. Whether it was developing new technologies to help businesses operate more efficiently or creating products and services that improved people's health and well-being, I was determined to leave a lasting mark on the world.

-Live ScreenTV

With a steady stream of revenue from our Sepal Reproductive Devices venture and various consulting projects, I finally had the freedom to focus my energy on getting Live Screen TV off the ground. This new endeavor would take me back to the city as we abandoned the comforts of the suburbs and embraced a new chapter in the heart of Boston.

The opportunity to dedicate my full attention to this exciting project was invigorating. Live Screen TV could be a game-changer, empowering anyone to create and share content innovatively. After years of juggling multiple ventures, I was eager to pour my passion and expertise into this new vision.

Of course, launching a startup from scratch would have its fair share of challenges, but the cash flow and stability I had built up in recent years gave me the confidence and resources to take this leap. As I set out to assemble the team and secure the necessary funding, I knew this could be the beginning of something truly remarkable - a chance to blaze a new trail in the rapidly evolving world of streaming digital media and content creation.

-Creating Multiple Opportunities

In 2003, my wife and I started Sepal Reproductive Devices. We represented a line of catheters from France. The company offered her a chance to be their exclusive/distributor representative. I was excited to learn so much about an industry where we assisted couples in getting pregnant!

The company sustained us nicely for the next ten years. We innovated a white-label/private-label pregnancy test, sold a test for early detection of fetal rupture, and offered fertility centers to sell it, making a very healthy margin.

Move back to the "LD."

I had enough of suburbia during this time and moved to downtown Boston. We bought a condo and rented an office in the Leather District. I returned to my roots. Something I had envisioned when I was a kid!

One of my new passions was providing clean drinking water for kids. I would try to bottle water from a resource in Colorado Springs and give it away! (My spiritual advisor had indicated I was to do "something with helping people get clean water.")

I was fortunate to meet another of my mentors, Henry "Bob" Hidell, at this event. He convinced me this was not feasible by pointing out many obstacles that would be challenging to overcome—I listened to him! We also had an immediate chemistry, and Bob invited me to join his team as an "entrepreneur in residence."

Bob had a client in mind on Long Island with whom he had a contract to provide all kinds of services. This was an excellent fit for me.

-Anecdote: Pure Safe Water /Incredible Trade Show Promo

I produced an award-winning video and ran a promotion that attracted over 6,000 visitors to our trade show booth. I served the attendees free coffee and cake for the afternoon show break. The custom cake was giant, shaped just like our water-purifying trailer. Additionally, I coordinated with other local businesses to create a network of services we could offer our clients. Our booth, the video, and people walking through our trailer—we were the show's big hit!

Part VI

Resilience Reborn 2013-2023

1. From the Ashes: Rebuilding My Life and Career

The decade spanning from 2013 to 2023 was a period of significant personal and professional challenges that tested my resilience and adaptability like never before. During this time, I faced the upheaval of a painful divorce, the loss of my mother, and the need to rebuild my life from scratch. Amidst these personal struggles, I also navigated the rapidly evolving landscape of technology and entrepreneurship, seeking new opportunities for growth and impact.

One of the most transformative experiences of this chapter in my life was the sudden and unexpected end of my 37-year marriage. The emotional toll of the divorce is also compounded by the practical challenges of starting over at the age of 65, with limited resources and a sense of uncertainty about the future.

However, through the support of loved ones and a determined spirit, I gradually began to piece my life back together, learning valuable lessons about resilience and the power of human connection.

As I grappled with the personal upheaval of divorce, I also found myself drawn to new entrepreneurial pursuits that aligned with my passions and values. Inspired by my mother's passing in a nursing home, I set out to create a virtual reality app designed to bring joy and connection to seniors in assisted living facilities. Despite the technical challenges and financial constraints, I assembled a dedicated team and poured my heart into developing a product that could make a real difference in people's lives.

2. Shock and Awe - Blindsided: Navigating the Upheaval of Divorce

As I stepped into my office conference room that fateful morning in 2013, I had no idea that my life was about to be turned upside down. I was riding high on the excitement of a new crowdfunding commitment for my latest venture, Live Screen TV, a platform designed to empower anyone to create and share their content. But instead of the team I expected to see, I was greeted by a room full of strangers who informed me that my wife was divorcing me.

Everything I had built over the past 35 years - my marriage, business, and sense of identity - came crashing down around me. I was given a restraining order and told to leave my home and my life as I knew it. That night, I slept in my car, wondering how I had gone from a successful entrepreneur to a homeless, jobless, and soon-to-be divorced man in the span of a few hours.

The months that followed were some of the darkest of my life. I moved in with my brother and sister-in-law, who showed me incredible kindness and support as I tried to pick up the pieces. My dear friend Mark Belenkii offered me a job as a limo driver. I got up at 3:00 AM to shuttle people to and from the airport, trying to make sense of my new reality. I was 65 years old, starting over from scratch, and wondering if I had anything left to give.

A good memory- I drove Patriots Star Julian Edelman around Boston on a Photoshoot for the NFL.

I remember those dark days like yesterday, the humbling fall from grace that shook me. Just a few months before, I'd been riding high, living the entrepreneur's dream in Boston - wine and dining, closing deals, thinking I had it all figured out. But pride comes before the fall, as they say, and man did I fall hard. *"You don't hear the shot that kills you !"*

Suddenly, I was dead broke with $600 and desperate, forced to swallow my pride and take any gig to keep the lights on. That's how I

found myself behind the wheel of a limo at 3 AM, ferrying people. !!!
Me, the high-flying entrepreneur, now just another bleary-eyed driver
grinding out a living on tips and fumes. But strangely, that limo gig
ended up being a lifeline. Sure, the hours were rough, but the pay with
tips was reasonable. At least it kept me afloat and gave me something to
hang onto while I figured out my next move. I learned so much from
the many conversations I had with passengers. We all have a story; I
saw firsthand how people framed their experiences and how alike most
people are.

Even more suddenly, I wasn't given access to any of my belongings
for over nine weeks. When I finally got my clothes, they did not fit as I
had lost about 40 lbs !! (The Irony)

And in the quiet moments between fares, I slowly began to make
peace with my new reality. This was my ground zero, rock bottom - the
only way out was up. I vowed to find a way to rebuild, no matter what
it took. That limo wasn't the end of my story; it was just the beginning
of a new chapter. And you know what? I was damn grateful to have it.

It was a bitter pill to swallow, watching my ego crumble in the
rearview mirror with each passing mile. The long, lonely nights gave
me plenty of time to wrestle with the doubts and recriminations that
haunted me. How had I fallen so far, so fast? Would I ever claw my way
back to where I'd been? The road ahead seemed long and dark, with no
end in sight.

-My Friend Carol Daniels

But despite my despair, I discovered a resilience and strength I
didn't know I possessed. With the help of an Angel, my friend Carol
Daniels, who cooked and took me out to dinners, bought me groceries,
bedding, towels, a gym membership, and reminded me to keep living,
I slowly began to rebuild.

-Anecdote Giving Back

The concept of "doing good, giving back without expectations,
unconditional love." I had previously met Carol in Sudbury when I had

failed in a venture. I could barely make rent, handle credit card debt, etc. I was in trouble. Indeed, I needed to find a new place to live and keep continuity in my life. I met Carol, and after I told her my story of needing a place to live, like now. She immediately went into action to save the day. It was late on a Friday, and the property owner was in California with a 3-hour time difference. Carol secured the house in just a few minutes, and we could occupy it the next day.

A few days later, after I had settled the family in new digs, My timing was a bit uncanny as I had reached out to thank her and buy a drink, but I found out that her husband had suddenly suffered a heart attack and passed away. I did not think about it. I immediately went to her home to help her family arrange food, transportation, logistics, etc. Carol and I had just met, and my kindness to her was offering her some form of comfort. She said I was an "Angel sent to her." So, when I was at my lowest, I reached out for a shoulder to cry on, and Carol was there for me. Today, we have a deep friendship with an uncanny, cherished connection!

-Navigating the Social Stigmas of Divorce, Aging, and Entrepreneurship

As I struggled to navigate the aftermath of my devastating divorce, I found myself suffocating under the oppressive weight of societal stigmas and prejudices. At age 65, I was forced to confront the daunting task of personally and professionally rebuilding my life from the ground up. With each step forward, I could feel the piercing gaze of judgment dull into my back, as if the world around me was quietly whispering, 'He's too old to start over, too tainted by his past failures to be taken seriously.'

But even as I grappled with the weight of these societal expectations, I could feel a fierce determination rising within me - a resolve to shatter the mold and rewrite the narrative of what it means to start over later in life. I refused to be defined by my age, my marital status, or my past setbacks. Instead, I channeled my energy into my entrepreneurial ventures, pouring my heart and soul into building something meaningful and impactful. With each small victory, each milestone achieved, I could feel the grip of those stigmas loosening, giving way to a renewed sense of purpose and possibility. I was determined to prove that reinvention knows no age limit and that the human spirit is capable of remarkable resilience and transformation."

I refused to accept those limiting beliefs. I knew in my bones that I still had so much left to give, so many dreams yet to chase. And so, with focus and determination, I set out to rewrite the narrative, to shatter the stereotypes that would seek to confine me.

In the face of my upheaval, I doubled down on my entrepreneurial pursuits, pouring my passion and creativity into new ventures that would allow me to make a tangible difference in the world. From the virtual reality app designed to combat loneliness in senior care facilities to the real estate imaging business I built from the ground up, I was driven by a sense of purpose that transcended the societal expectations thrust upon me.

And you know what? In doing so, I found that I wasn't just defying the norms - I was tapping into a wellspring of resilience and adaptability forged over a lifetime of ups and downs. The lessons I had learned, the failures I had weathered, and the reinventions I had undergone coalesced into a unique set of skills and insights that allowed me to navigate the ever-changing entrepreneurship landscape with a level of agility that left many of my younger counterparts in awe.

To be sure, the road has been challenging. Judgment, doubts, and moments of self-recrimination have all been constant companions on this journey. But with each obstacle, I've overcome and each milestone I've achieved, I've grown more vital, resilient, and determined to prove that age is nothing but a number and that divorce is not a scarlet letter to be borne in shame.

This is the true essence of my story - not just the tale of an entrepreneur but of a human being who has refused to be defined by societal expectations or the trials life has thrown his way. It is a testament to the power of the human spirit and the transformative potential within us, regardless of our age, relationship status, or the conventional wisdom that would seek to constrain us.

3. Rising from the Ashes: Discovering New Purpose

I started dating again, navigating the unfamiliar world of online dating and learning to open my heart after so much pain. And eventually, I found "love" again with an incredible woman named Lucy, who has been my partner and rock ever since.

But my journey was far from over. As I grappled with the fallout of a brutal divorce that left me with almost nothing, I also found myself driven by a new sense of purpose. When my mother passed away in a nursing home, I was struck by the isolation and loneliness that so many seniors experience in their final years. As a technologist and an innovator, I knew there had to be a better way.

And so, with no money and resources, I built a virtual reality app that could bring joy, connection, and meaning to the lives of seniors in assisted living facilities. I poured my heart and soul into creating something extraordinary. I faced countless challenges and setbacks, from technical hurdles to the devastating impact of the COVID-19 pandemic, but I have never given up.

Along the way, I also started a side business called RealTView, which used 3D imaging to create virtual tours for real estate agents. Starting with only $3000 a camera and a dream, I grew the business to over $260,000 in revenue in just three years, only to see it come to a grinding halt when the pandemic hit.

I sold the company in 2022.

But through it all, I learned that success is not about the destination but the journey. It's about the relationships we build, the lives we touch, and the difference we make along the way. It's about finding purpose and meaning in the face of adversity and never losing sight of what truly matters.

Looking back on the past decade, I am grateful for the lessons I have learned and the person I have become. I have faced some of the darkest moments but also discovered a resilience and strength I never knew I possessed. I have lost everything but also gained a new perspective on what truly matters in life.

So, to anyone reading this who may be facing struggles and setbacks, I want to offer this message of hope: no matter how old or how many times you have been knocked down, it is never too late to start over. Finding your purpose, building something meaningful, and making a difference in the world is always possible.

The road may be extended, and the obstacles may seem impossible, but I promise you this: if you keep putting one foot in front of the other if you surround yourself with people who believe in you, and if you never lose sight of what truly matters, you will find your way. You will rise from the ashes, stronger and more resilient than ever.

Looking back on your journey, as I am doing now, you will see that every struggle, setback, and moment of despair was simply a stepping stone to becoming the person you were always meant to be. So keep going, keep believing, and never give up on yourself. The best is yet to come.

-Adding Humor to the Mix

Throughout my life, humor has served me well on almost all occasions. Whether in a professional or personal setting, I've Found That Using humor to connect with people is an effective way to break the ice and create a comfortable atmosphere.

I've found that humor is an excellent tool for helping me connect with people and establish trust. When I Speak with someone, whether a prospect or a new colleague, I often use humor to let their guard down. If I can make someone laugh, even for a second, it's usually enough to create a moment of connection and open up the possibility for further dialogue.

I have found that humor can be a powerful tool for breaking down barriers and making connections in business and personal interactions. Humor allows me to approach people who may have enormous resumes and extensive expertise with a degree of lightness and informality.

For example, when I meet someone, I'll joke and say something like, "Please explain to me.... I read your bio... how did you get to be such an underachiever?" delivered funnily and sarcastically). It's my way of breaking the ice and showing that I don't take myself too seriously.

I've found that using humor in this way has often led to many conversations starting this way. It has helped me establish a connection, build rapport, and lead the conversation into areas I'm curious about. It's been an effective tool, and I always use it when meeting people and prospects for the first time.

In addition to using humor, being purposely provocative can be an effective conversation starter. I've used this approach in various situations, especially when meeting new people and being asked about my profession.

I stood next to one of my mentors, Stan Sidman, at networking events; Stan, with a very straight face and serious delivery, would tell people when we met them, "I have just been released from jail and was looking for a gig to get back in the community." This would often lead to surprised and curious looks on their faces, but it was an effective way to break the ice and start a conversation. It also elicited a tremendous amount of laughter. I have used this approach. It is always a kick and a great way to see if someone is listening. Try it!

This approach may not be suitable for all people and situations, but it's been a way for me to be authentic and break the monotony of small talk. I've found that being bold and daring can be a great conversation starter and make people feel more comfortable opening up. I also used it to showcase the authenticity and comfort of my skin.

I've done this countless times, laughed a lot, and made myriad connections, and it's always been a conversation starter. It allowed me to be different and make a memorable impression. I would then steer the conversation towards something more serious or professional. It helped me establish trust and a sense of humor, which makes people feel at ease.

4."Riding the Wave of Innovation

"Riding the Wave of Innovation: The path of entrepreneurship is not for the faint of heart. It demands dedication, perseverance, and sacrifices that can only be truly understood through firsthand experience. One of the most significant sacrifices I've had to make as an entrepreneur is time. The journey to a successful business often involves working long hours, missing out on precious moments with loved ones, and forgoing weekends and holidays to pursue your vision.

It's a hard truth to face, but the reality is that as an entrepreneur, your time is often not your own. You're at the mercy of deadlines, client demands, and the never-ending list of tasks that come with running a business.

Another major sacrifice is financial security. When starting a business, you often invest your money and resources without guaranteeing success. This can be a terrifying prospect, especially when you have a family to support and bills to pay. I've had to take on debt, dip into my savings, and make difficult choices about where to allocate limited funds, all while knowing that there's a chance the business might not make it.

Despite these sacrifices, I've learned that the key to success is staying focused, determined, and committed to your goals. Sometimes, you want to give up when the obstacles seem impossible, and the stress feels overwhelming. But in those moments, you must dig deep and find the strength to keep pushing forward.

One of the most important things I've learned is that there is never a "good time" to start a company. If you wait for the perfect moment, you'll be waiting forever. There will always be reasons to put it off, to say "maybe next year" or "when the kids are older." But the truth is, if you have a vision and a passion, you owe it to yourself to pursue it.

That being said, I've also realized the importance of prioritizing family time. As much as I love my work, my family is the foundation upon which everything else is built. I've had to learn to be more present, to put down the phone, close the laptop, and give my full attention to the people who matter most. It's not always easy, but it's always worth it.

Looking back, I can honestly say that the sacrifices I've made as an entrepreneur have been some of my life's most challenging and rewarding experiences. They've taught me resilience, adaptability, and the true meaning of hard work. And while I may have missed out on some things along the way, I know that the legacy I'm building and the impact I'm making is worth every sacrifice."

-Capital to Grow

One of the most critical lessons I've learned in my entrepreneurial journey is the importance of having sufficient capital to support the growth of your business. It's a lesson that many entrepreneurs, myself included, often learn the hard way. In the early days of starting a business, it's easy to underestimate how much money you'll need to keep things running smoothly, especially when unexpected challenges arise.

I've found that having a cushion of capital is essential for growth and survival. When times get tough, as they inevitably do, having a financial safety net can mean the difference between weathering the storm and going under. During these challenging periods, many businesses fail because they don't have the resources to keep going.

I advise aspiring entrepreneurs to overestimate their capital needs consistently. Take the number you think you'll require and double it. It may seem excessive, but it's better to have too much than too little. You never know when an unexpected expense or a promising opportunity will require a significant investment.

Of course, securing that capital is often easier said than done. That's why it's so important to always be in the mindset of creating sales, raising money, and generating enthusiasm for your business. Whether you're talking to potential investors, customers, or partners, you need to be able to passionately convey your vision and belief in what you're doing.

One strategy that has worked well for me is to think of myself as a seed planter. I'm constantly cultivating relationships and planting the seeds of future opportunities, even if they don't immediately bear fruit. By developing a solid network and consistently nurturing those connections, I can tap into a wealth of resources and support when I need it most.

But even with the best planning and preparation, the road to success is rarely smooth. I've had months where everything seemed to be going perfectly, only to be followed by months where it felt like everything was falling apart. The key is staying focused on your long-term goals and maintaining a positive attitude despite setbacks.

It's also important to remember that raising capital often means giving up a portion of ownership in your company. But the truth is, having a smaller piece of a much larger pie is almost always better than having a large piece of a tiny pie.

Ultimately, deciding to bring on investors or partners is profoundly personal and depends on your unique circumstances and goals. Regardless of your path, the importance of sufficient capital must be balanced. It's the fuel that allows your business to grow, adapt, and thrive, even in the face of inevitable challenges."

-**Starting a Business with No Funding**

Starting a business without the safety net of investor funding or significant personal financial resources can be a daunting prospect. It requires creativity, resourcefulness, and sheer determination. When I first embarked on my entrepreneurial journey, I found myself standing at the precipice of a daunting challenge: starting a business without the comfort of investor backing or a substantial personal financial cushion.

It was a prospect that demanded an unwavering commitment to creativity, resourcefulness, and tenacity—qualities I would discover were essential to my success but not always easy to summon. Yet, for those brave enough to take the leap and embrace the trials and tribulations of this path, the rewards can be truly transformative. Everyone possesses. But for those willing to take on the challenge, the rewards can be immeasurable.

One of the most effective strategies I found was to network relentlessly. I attended every industry event, conference, and meetup I could find to connect with potential customers, partners, and mentors. I made it a point to listen more than I spoke, to ask questions, and to learn from those who had already succeeded in my field.

Through these relationships, I gained valuable insights into the needs and challenges of my target market. I used this knowledge to develop products and services that solved real problems and provided tangible value to my customers. By focusing on creating value rather than just making a quick sale, I built a loyal customer base and generated steady revenue streams.

Another critical aspect of starting a business without funding is being resourceful and finding creative ways to reduce costs and maximize efficiency. This meant leveraging technology and virtual tools wherever possible rather than investing in expensive physical infrastructure. It also meant being willing to wear many hats and take on tasks that might typically be outsourced or delegated in a larger organization.

However, the most essential qualities for any entrepreneur with limited resources are sheer determination and grit. There will be countless obstacles and setbacks along the way, and it's easy to get discouraged when progress is slow, or things don't go according to plan. The key is staying focused on your vision and pushing forward, even when the odds are stacked against you.

In those early days, I had to think outside the box constantly. I remember one particular instance when I needed to secure a crucial piece of equipment for my fledgling business, but I lacked the funds to purchase it outright. Instead of giving up, I reached out to my network and found someone willing to lend me the equipment in exchange for a percentage of my future profits. It was a creative solution that allowed me to move forward without compromising my limited financial resources. This experience taught me that resourcefulness and the willingness to ask for help can be just as valuable as capital when starting a business."

One of the most valuable lessons I learned during this time was the importance of adaptability and adaptability to change. In the early days of a business, it's common to have a specific idea of what your product or service will look like and how the market will receive it. However, the reality is often quite different, and being willing to pivot and adjust your approach based on feedback and data is essential for long-term success.

Starting a business without funding is not for the faint of heart. It requires a unique combination of skill, creativity, and tenacity that only some possess. But the rewards can be life-changing for those willing to take on the challenge and work hard. It's incredible to reflect on what you've built and know you did it all through your efforts and determination.

Of course, it's essential to recognize that not every business can or should start without adequate funding. There are certain situations where outside investment is necessary or advantageous. But for many entrepreneurs, especially those just starting, bootstrapping can be an excellent way to maintain control over their vision and build a solid foundation for future growth.

Ultimately, starting a business with or without funding is profoundly personal and depends on your unique goals, circumstances, and risk tolerance. Regardless of your path, the key is to stay focused on creating value, building relationships, and never giving up on your dreams. Anything is possible with hard work, determination, and a willingness to learn and adapt."

-Isolation - Home Alone

In the early days of my entrepreneurial journey, I was intoxicated by the promise of freedom that came with being my boss. However, as I settled into the daily grind of running a business from my tiny home office, the harsh realities of isolation quickly began to set in. Gone were the lively interactions and bustling energy of a shared workspace; instead, I was engulfed in a deafening silence, my only companions being the stoic potted plants that lined my windowsill. It was a far cry from the glamorous lifestyle I had envisioned when I first set out on this path, and I soon realized that the actual price of freedom was often paid in solitude.

But as I pressed on, I discovered that isolation didn't have to be a curse; instead, it could be an opportunity for growth and self-discovery. I reflected on my priorities, values, and goals in the quiet moments between the endless tasks and responsibilities. I learned to embrace solitude as a chance to focus inward to cultivate a stronger sense of self-awareness and resilience. As I did so, I slowly began to build a network of like-minded entrepreneurs who understood this path's unique challenges and triumphs. Together, we formed a community of support and collaboration, proving that connection and growth are always possible, even in isolation.

-Anecdote - Jen and the Stereo

My oldest daughter was over 18 months old when we lived in Chestnut Hill. She was a very active and curious toddler. One day, she climbed up one of our bookcases and accidentally pulled the stereo receiver down, which fell on her nose. Fortunately, I was home then and could provide immediate care for her. I quickly got her to the hospital, where she received stitches for her injury. In this case, it was good that I was present at home to handle the situation promptly and ensure she got the medical attention needed.

But you know what I've learned over the years? Isolation doesn't have to be a bad thing. It can be an opportunity to grow in ways you never thought possible. When you're forced to rely on yourself and figure things out independently, you develop a scrappy, can-do attitude essential for success as an entrepreneur.

Of course, that doesn't mean you have to go entirely alone. One of the best things I ever did for myself and my business was actively seeking opportunities to connect with other entrepreneurs who got it. I started attending networking events and conferences; I joined online communities and forums where I could ask questions and get advice from people who had been there and done that.

And you know what? It was like a whole new world opened up to me. Suddenly, this fantastic group of people understood what I was going through. They were there to celebrate my wins, commiserate over my losses, and offer guidance when I felt stuck. It reminded me that even though I was technically working alone, I was never truly alone in this journey.

And let's not forget about the elephant in the room – the COVID-19 pandemic. Talk about isolation, right? Suddenly, even those used to working remotely felt more disconnected than ever. But here's the thing – this is where that adaptability and flexibility I mentioned earlier really come into play. Maybe it means finding new ways to collaborate with your team over Zoom or pivoting your business to meet the changing needs of your customers. It's not always easy, but it is essential to stay open to new possibilities and be willing to roll with the punches.

Being a solo entrepreneur is not for the faint of heart. It takes guts, grit, and a whole lot of hustle. But it's also an incredible opportunity to learn more about yourself, push past your limits, and create something unique. So, if you're feeling isolated right now, know you're not alone. Reach out, build those relationships, and keep on keeping on. You've got this!

Part VII

Wisdom for Aspiring Entrepreneurs

I've learned one fundamental truth throughout my decades-long entrepreneurial journey. In that case, it is this: the path to lasting success is paved not just with strategy and execution but with an unshakable mindset that guides our every step. How we approach challenges, setbacks, and opportunities ultimately determines our ability to turn dreams into reality and build thriving businesses.

As the founder of multiple ventures, I have weathered my fair share of shit storms - moments where the obstacles seemed impossible and the future uncertain. But in those crucible experiences, I have discovered the true power of mindset, the way it can transform adversity into triumph and limitation into possibility.

Time and again, I have witnessed how a committed, positive mindset can Propel an entrepreneur forward, even in the face of daunting circumstances. It is the unwavering belief in one's abilities, the relentless determination to push past roadblocks, and the flexibility to adapt and pivot when necessary. These qualities separate those who merely dream of success from those who go on to shape it.

As I reflect on the entrepreneurial journey that has spanned my career, I'm struck by how dramatically the landscape has transformed—not just in terms of the technologies and business models but also in the infrastructure and support systems available to founders like myself.

When I started, the path to entrepreneurship felt far more solitary and resource-constrained. Access to capital was limited, often requiring tireless networking, the willingness to leverage personal savings, or the ability to convince traditional lenders and investors to take a chance on unproven ideas. The notion of crowdfunding platforms, angel networks, and venture capital firms scouring the landscape for the next big thing was virtually unheard of.

And the mentorship opportunities were few and far between. Sure, I had my fair share of seasoned veterans who took me under their wing, sharing invaluable lessons and opening doors that may have remained closed. But the idea of structured incubator and accelerator programs designed to nurture and scale young businesses? That was still firmly in the realm of science fiction.

Even the cultural perceptions of entrepreneurship have undergone a dramatic shift. Gone are the days when striking out on one's own was viewed with a wary eye as a risky proposition relegated to society's oddballs and mavericks. Today, entrepreneurship has been elevated to near-mythical status, with founders celebrated as visionaries, innovators, and disruptors—the engine of economic progress and technological advancement.

Of course, this transformation has come with its own set of challenges. The democratization of entrepreneurship has also brought about a dizzying level of competition as countless startups jockey for attention, resources, and market share. The pressure to scale rapidly, today ahead of emerging trends, and constantly reinvent one's business model - is enough to make one's head spin.

But these changes, for all their disruption, have ultimately been a net positive. By lowering the barriers to entry and providing a rich tapestry of support systems, the entrepreneurial ecosystem has opened the door for a more diverse array of founders to pursue their dreams. And that diversity, in turn, has fueled innovation, challenged the status quo, and pushed the boundaries of what's possible.

As I've navigated this evolving landscape, I've had to continuously adapt my mindset and toolkit. The skills and strategies that may have worked in my early days are often woefully inadequate for the realities of today's business world. Remaining agile, curious, and committed to lifelong learning has become essential, as it can tap into the wealth of resources and communities now available to entrepreneurs. Today, I am actively participating in online and in-person events. I am always encouraged when I see other entrepreneurs navigating and seeking mentors open to collaboration.

Indeed, this very adaptability - this willingness to evolve alongside the ecosystem - has been one of the defining hallmarks of my entrepreneurial journey. As I look to the future, I'm excited to see how the landscape will continue transforming, opening up new avenues for creativity, impact, and success. Ultimately, entrepreneurship's true power lies not in the individual but in the collective spirit of those who dare to dream, innovate, and forge their paths.

Of course, cultivating such a mindset is challenging. It requires a constant commitment to self-reflection, growth, and the willingness to confront our limiting beliefs. However, the results can be remarkable when we harness the transformative power of mindset.

Whether it was summoning the courage to launch a bold new venture in the face of personal upheaval or tapping into my creativity to identify innovative solutions to complex challenges, my mindset has been the guiding light that has kept me moving forward, no matter the obstacles.

It is a lesson to impart to every aspiring entrepreneur who reads these words - that the true secret to success lies not just in technical mastery or resource acquisition but in the ability to forge an unbreakable mindset of resilience, adaptability, and unwavering self-belief.

1. From Brick and Mortar to the Digital Age: The Evolution of Entrepreneurship

Starting a business in the 1980s and '90s was a more challenging prospect than today without the benefit of digital tools and platforms. Many tasks that are now automated or streamlined require significant time and manual effort. The business's administrative burdens could be overwhelming, from bookkeeping and accounting to marketing and customer relationship management.

This often meant starting small and lean, bootstrapping your way to success through hard work, creativity, and sheer determination. It requires a willingness to take calculated risks and make the most of limited resources, finding innovative ways to get your product or service in front of potential customers.

Another significant challenge was the limited access to information and expertise. In the pre-internet era, finding mentors, advisors, or basic information about starting and running a business could be daunting. It often meant relying on books, workshops, or personal networks to fill in the gaps and provide guidance.

But despite these challenges, there were also some advantages to starting a business in the 80s and 90s. For one, the competitive landscape was often less crowded, with fewer players vying for market share in many industries. This could make it easier to differentiate your offering and build a loyal customer base.

Additionally, the pace of business moved more slowly in many ways, allowing for more time to plan, strategize, and build relationships with key stakeholders. The emphasis on in-person networking and relationship-building could lead to more robust, enduring partnerships and collaborations.

Contrast this with the business landscape of today, where the barriers to entry for starting a business are significantly lowered. The widespread availability of digital tools and platforms has made it easier to start and scale a business from anywhere in the world, often with minimal upfront investment.

From online marketplaces and e-commerce platforms to social media and digital marketing tools, entrepreneurs today have access to many resources and channels for reaching and engaging with customers. The ability to automate and streamline many business processes has freed up time and energy to focus on core competencies and value creation.

At the same time, the landscape has become increasingly crowded and competitive, with new players emerging all the time. The speed of technological change and the pressure to innovate and adapt can be relentless, requiring a constant focus on learning, growth, and evolution.

In many ways, the key to success in today's business landscape is similar to what it was in the 80s and 90s: a combination of hard work, creativity, and the willingness to take calculated risks. But the tools, resources, and channels available to entrepreneurs have expanded exponentially, creating new opportunities and challenges at every turn.

As I reflect on my journey and the lessons I've learned, I'm struck by how much the world of entrepreneurship has changed, yet how much remains the same. Building a successful business – identifying a need, creating value, and delivering on your promises – remains as important as ever. However, how we achieve those goals has evolved and expanded in ways that would have been hard to imagine just a few decades ago.

For aspiring entrepreneurs today, the key is to embrace the tools and resources available while staying true to the timeless principles of hard work, creativity, and perseverance. By combining the best of both worlds—the innovative spirit of the past with the technological advantages of the present—you can build a business that succeeds and thrives in the face of change and uncertainty."

2. In It for the Long Run: Cultivating Endurance and Resilience

Alright, when setting the vision and milestones for a project or venture, it's crucial to embrace divergent thinking and be willing to tackle problems head-on. I've learned that it's easy to fall into the trap of "stinking thinking," where you get bogged down by negative thoughts and roadblocks. But the key is to **shift your mindset and focus on making things happen, no matter what.**

Setting a vision and milestones is all about having a clear roadmap and staying focused on the end goal. It's not always easy, but embracing divergent thinking, staying customer-centric, and leveraging data-driven insights can create a plan that sets you up for success. And remember - even if you hit a few bumps along the way, just keep pushing forward and trust in the process. You've got this!

-Visionary and Disruptor: The Dual Mantles of the Entrepreneur

At the heart of every successful entrepreneurial journey lies the ability to see what others do not - envisioning a future that defies convention and challenges the status quo. As a founder, this dual role of visionary and disruptor is your most vital responsibility, for it is the driving force that shapes the direction and trajectory of your business.

Your strategic mind identifies unmet needs and untapped opportunities, your creative spark breathes life into innovative solutions, and your unwavering determination propels you to chart a course that may seem risky or unconventional to the outside world but which you know, in your core, holds the potential for transformative change.

I have walked this path myself, time and again, daring to dream beyond the confines of the familiar. Whether it was envisioning a groundbreaking VR app to combat loneliness in assisted living facilities or pioneering new approaches to document management and data processing, I have never been one to shy away from the road less traveled. It is in these uncharted territories that the most remarkable breakthroughs are born.

Of course, being a visionary and a disruptor is a challenging feat. It requires a unique blend of skills—from keen market analysis and strategic foresight to the courage to challenge assumptions and take calculated risks. At times, it may even mean standing firm in the face of skepticism or resistance, trusting in the power of your vision to ultimately rise above the naysayers.

But the rewards are immeasurable for those who have embraced this dual calling. In shaping the future, we leave an indelible mark on the world, creating products, services, and experiences that improve lives, drive innovation, and inspire others to reach the seemingly impossible.

-Adaptability/Pivoting/Learning from failure

Of course, visioning is not a one-time exercise. It requires ongoing reflection, refinement, and adaptation as circumstances change and new challenges emerge. This is where adaptability becomes crucial. As a founder, you must be able to pivot and adjust your strategy as needed while staying true to your core mission and values.

One of the most important aspects of adaptability is the ability to learn from failure. No founder or business gets it right every time, and the most successful entrepreneurs can often turn setbacks into opportunities for growth and improvement. This requires a mindset of continuous learning, a willingness to experiment and iterate, and the resilience to bounce back from disappointment. Remember, you are always young enough to get advice from a mentor.

Another essential quality of influential founders is the ability to build and lead strong teams. *No entrepreneur can succeed alone,* and the most visionary leaders can often surround themselves with talented, motivated individuals who share their passion and purpose. This means identifying and cultivating potential, creating a culture of collaboration and accountability, and empowering team members to take ownership and initiative.

Ultimately, the role of a founder is to create something valuable and enduring. Whether it's a product, a service, or an entire company, your vision gives your business its purpose and impact. It inspires others to join you on your journey and drives you to keep pushing forward in the face of challenges and setbacks.

But it's important to remember that visioning is not just about the destination but also the journey. Bringing a vision to life – turning an idea into a reality – is often just as rewarding as the result. It's the opportunity to create something new, to make a difference in the world, and to leave a lasting legacy.

Reflecting on my journey as a disruptor, founder, and visionary, I'm struck by how much I've learned and grown. Each phase has brought unique challenges and opportunities from the early days of bootstrapping and experimentation to the later stages of scaling and expansion. But through it all, the power of a clear and compelling vision has been the constant thread, guiding me forward and inspiring me to keep reaching new heights.

By sharing my experiences and insights, I aim to inspire and empower other founders to embrace their visionary potential. Whether you're just starting on your entrepreneurial journey or a seasoned veteran, the ability to envision and create something remarkable is within your grasp. All it takes is the courage to dream big, the willingness to take action, and the perseverance to see it through."

-Forging Greatness as a Solo Entrepreneur

As an experienced solo entrepreneur, I've had to continuously evolve and refine my entrepreneurial toolkit's tools, strategies, and skills. While the fundamental principles that have guided me - perseverance, adaptability, and a relentless pursuit of innovation - have remained constant, the specific application and implementation of these qualities have had to adapt to the changing market conditions and technological advancements over the decades.

Take networking, for example. In my early days, building connections and cultivating relationships was about face-to-face interactions, attending industry events, and leveraging my personal Rolodex. But as the digital landscape has exploded, I've had to learn how to navigate online communities, optimize my social media presence, and leverage data-driven insights to identify and engage with the right potential partners and customers.

Similarly, my approach to sales and marketing has undergone a dramatic transformation. Gone are the days of cold-calling from printed directories and relying solely on my powers of persuasion. Now, I'm leveraging sophisticated customer relationship management (CRM) tools, deploying targeted digital campaigns, and using data analytics to understand better and serve my target markets' evolving needs.

Even my project management techniques have had to adapt to the realities of remote work, distributed teams, and the need for more agile, iterative methodologies. I've had to become fluent in the latest collaboration software, project tracking systems, and Agile frameworks - skills that would have been entirely foreign to me in the early stages of my entrepreneurial journey.

As I've grown my businesses, I've also had to expand my toolkit regarding financial management, human resources, and legal compliance. The days of relying solely on my scrappy, jack-of-all-trades approach have given way to the need for more specialized expertise and the strategic delegation of tasks to skilled professionals.

But through it all, I've maintained a steadfast commitment to continuous learning and adaptation. I've never been one to rest on my laurels or assume that the strategies that worked yesterday will be sufficient for tomorrow. Instead, I'm constantly scanning the horizon identifying new tools and best practices, and experimenting to find the most effective ways to bring my entrepreneurial vision to life.

It's a never-ending process, to be sure, but one that I've come to embrace as an essential part of the entrepreneurial experience. After all, in a world that is changing at a breakneck pace, the ability to evolve and refine one's toolkit is not just a nice-to-have - it's a fundamental necessity for sustained success and impact.

As a solo entrepreneur, I've learned that the road to greatness is paved with vision, determination, and mastery of daily discipline and self-care. When you're the sole driving force behind your business, it can be easy to become consumed by endless tasks and demands, losing sight of the bigger picture and the importance of balance.

Yet, the true greatness of the solo entrepreneur is born in cultivating this delicate equilibrium - between laser-sharp focus and restorative respite. By breaking down my work into manageable chunks and consciously stepping away and recharging, I've found that I'm more productive, inspired, and resilient in the face of challenges.

Of course, maintaining this level of discipline and self-awareness isn't always easy. There are days when the siren call of overwork and burnout can be noisy, tempting me to push myself beyond my limits. But I've learned that true greatness isn't about endless hours and a relentless grind but the ability to harness my energy, creativity, and passion sustainably.

That's why I regularly inject moments of curiosity, exploration, and joy into my everyday life—whether pursuing a new hobby, engaging in thought-provoking conversations, or simply taking a stroll to clear my mind. The seeds of my most incredible ideas and breakthroughs often take root in these rejuvenating spaces. You must incorporate the time to refresh.

Ultimately, the path to greatness as a solo entrepreneur is not about heroic feats or grandiose achievements but the quiet mastery of the fundamental building blocks of success: discipline, self-care, and a relentless commitment to growth and evolution. By honoring these principles, I've reached new heights in my professional endeavors and maintained a deep sense of fulfillment and purpose in my personal life.

3. The Entrepreneurial Marathon - Pacing Yourself for the Long Haul

As I look back on my decades-long entrepreneurial journey, I've come to appreciate how much of a marathon it truly is. When I first started, I'll admit I had this romantic notion that success would come quickly - if I just worked hard enough, put in the long hours, and chased every opportunity, the accolades and riches would soon follow. Boy, was I in for a rude awakening?

The reality is that entrepreneurship is a grueling test of endurance, resilience, and self-discipline. It's not a sprint but a relentless, ever-evolving race that demands you pace yourself, strategize carefully, and learn to manage your energy and resources with laser-like precision. There have been many times when I've felt like throwing in the towel when the obstacles seemed impossible, and the finish line was nowhere in sight.

But throughout it all, I've learned that the valid key to success isn't just about working harder than everyone else - it's about working smarter. It's about cultivating the mental toughness to weather the storms, the adaptability to navigate shifting terrain, and the self-awareness to recognize when to slow down, recharge, and refocus.

One of the biggest lessons I've learned is the importance of work-life balance. In the early days, I'll confess, I was the quintessential workaholic—chaining myself to my desk, skipping meals, and sacrificing precious family time, all in the name of my entrepreneurial ambitions. And you know what? It nearly broke me. I burned out, my health suffered, and I found myself making poor decisions that threatened to derail everything I'd worked so hard to build.

That's when I realized I needed to reframe my mindset - to stop viewing entrepreneurship as a series of all-or-nothing sprints and start approaching it as a lifelong journey that required a measured, sustainable pace. I began carving out sacred time for rest, reflection, and reconnection with the people and activities that nourished my soul. I learned to delegate more and to let go of the notion that I had to control every aspect of my business.

And you know what? It made all the difference. By taking a more holistic, balanced approach, I wasn't just avoiding burnout—I was becoming more productive, creative, and effective in my decision-making. The marathon mindset allowed me to stay nimble, adapt quickly to changing conditions, and keep my eyes fixed firmly on the horizon rather than just the immediate obstacles.

Of course, that's not to say the journey has been easy. Plenty of times, I've had to gut it out, push through the pain and fatigue, and keep moving forward. But I've learned to embrace those challenges, to view them as opportunities for growth and character-building rather than roadblocks to be feared.

Entrepreneurship isn't a sprint—it's a lifelong pursuit. The true winners aren't the ones who burn brightest but can sustain their momentum and pace themselves for the long haul. I try to impart this lesson to every aspiring founder I mentor because I know firsthand how crucial it is to maintain professional success, personal fulfillment, and well-being.

So, if there's one piece of advice I could offer to my fellow entrepreneurs, it would be this: Embrace the marathon mindset. Slow down, care for yourself, and keep your eyes fixed on the horizon. The finish line may be far in the distance, but if you can learn to manage your energy and resources with wisdom and discipline, I promise you, the rewards will be well worth the wait.

-Navigating Uncertainty

As an entrepreneur, I've come to accept uncertainty as my constant companion—an unwavering presence that sometimes feels like an oppressive weight upon my shoulders. The wise words of Rabbi Lord Jonathan Sacks often echo in my mind during these moments of doubt:

'Faith is not certainty; it means the courage to live with uncertainty.' And in entrepreneurship, courage is not just a virtue; it's a necessity.

We are all naturally averse to risk, preferring the comforts of the known over the uncertainty of the new. But it is in embracing that discomfort, in honing our ability to navigate the unknown, that we find our greatest strength. To do anything truly innovative, we must face uncertainty head-on, drawing upon our resilience and adaptability to forge a path forward.

When self-doubt and fear threaten to overwhelm us, we have a choice: to succumb to the paralysis of uncertainty or to rise above it with a clarity of purpose and a commitment to our vision. Do we let the fear of the unknown hold us back, or do we have the courage to invest in our future, trusting that the path will reveal itself?

The truth is, we are all wired for possibility. Our minds are brimming with worlds of potential waiting to be explored. And it is often through the crucible of uncertainty that the most remarkable breakthroughs and innovations emerge. By embracing the discomfort and becoming skilled at navigating the unknown, we open ourselves to the transformative power of new ideas and fresh perspectives.

-Anecdote: Mindset!

At a trade show, I talked with a young man struggling to find his path. I shared with him the importance of reframing one's story and focusing on the lessons learned from challenges and setbacks. By shifting our mindset and embracing a growth-oriented perspective, we can transform even the most difficult experiences into opportunities for learning and self-discovery.

He was very chatty and open. He told me he was transitioning but felt he had made many mistakes with his career. He had been working for a hedge fund, made lots of money, and left for a food service industry job, and was unhappy. Lost and uncertain of how to navigate his future

As a rule, I never invite myself to offer any advice or uninvited coaching, but in this case, I provided or asked if he would like some feedback and told him what I heard him say. I mentioned that he came off with self-loathing and pity for himself because he sees himself as a loser. -**Mindset!**

I turned to him and was very direct. and said, "What would this look and sound like if you reframed the story?" "Tell me that story about how much you learned from these experiences and how you will leverage your skills for the next journey. Reframe the story so you set yourself up for success. "Trust what you say and how your project will come together. Trust that it will! -**Mindset!**

4. Earning My Stripes: Hard-Won Lessons from the Trenches

During my start-up journey, I enrolled in the esteemed "School of Hard Knox." And let me tell you, I've got a few hard-earned degrees from this institution.

There's the good ol' FcukU, where I learned that sometimes you just gotta say "screw you" to the status quo. Then there's Screw You University, where I mastered the art of navigating the delightfully "fucked-up" landscape of entrepreneurship.

And who could forget Upa US, the distinguished degree program from the upper part of the country? Throw a Ph.D. from the illustrious Bend-Dover University, and you have a resume.

Of course, I've also picked up a few specialized certifications: Lawyer Up- U 93a, I Can Fire You, and the ever-popular I Fired You... Sue U. And let's not forget about Bankrupt U, where I learned that sometimes you just have to let the whole damn thing come crashing down.

Other degrees include It's the Economy, Crash U, and Crush U, to name a few. I've been navigating the unknown variables of the economy, walking that tightrope with no net below. It's been a wild ride, let me tell you. From the 11-month recession of '69-'70 to the 18-month slog of 2007-2009, COVID-19! I thought I had seen it all. WRONG! And you know what they say—what doesn't kill you makes you stronger.

While the "School of Hard Knox" may not be the most prestigious institution, it's undoubtedly equipped me with the skills and resilience to weather any storm. And trust me, you'll need a thick skin and a lot of grit regarding entrepreneurship. It's a good thing I've got both in spades.

5. Intuition and Improvisation: Trusting My Instincts in the Face of Uncertainty"

OK, now that my sales efforts with private label computers are over, I am looking for new opportunities and networking meetings.

I am worried about making mortgages and payments for the new BMW car. The impact of my financial loss was on the edge of being catastrophic. This caused undue stress and led me to make further poor decisions that quickly affected all areas of my life,

When my back was against the wall, and I had seemingly no answers to a desperately needed problem, I discovered that there was always an answer.

As I navigated the ups and downs of entrepreneurship, I began to develop a keen sense of the qualities necessary for success. I learned to trust my instincts, take calculated risks, and embrace the power of networking. I discovered that the most successful entrepreneurs could adapt quickly to changing market conditions, identify and capitalize on emerging trends, and build strong relationships with clients, partners, and investors.

As I reflect on this chapter in my life, I realize that my entrepreneurial journey was not just about building successful companies but about building character. Each challenge I faced, setback I encountered, and triumph I celebrated shaped me into the resilient, adaptable, and tenacious entrepreneur I am today.

Part VIII

Resilience Reborn Again

Just as I was brimming with excitement and optimism for the next chapter of my entrepreneurial journey, life had other plans. The wheels had barely begun turning on my ambitious Live-Screen TV project when the unthinkable happened—my wife abruptly filed for divorce, shattering the very foundation upon which I had built my life and livelihood.

In the span of a single afternoon, I went from a confident, driven business owner to a homeless, jobless, and soon-to-be divorced man, stripped of nearly everything I had spent decades building. As I sat alone in my car that fateful night, staring into the void, I couldn't help but wonder: how had it all come crashing down so quickly?

The following years would test me in ways I never imagined. Personal upheaval gave way to professional challenges as I navigated the rapidly evolving technology landscape, searching for new avenues to apply my skills and passions. But at every turn, another obstacle would arise, threatening to derail my efforts and leave me adrift in a sea of uncertainty.

Looking back, I realize that this moment was not just a turning point in my journey but a testament to the indomitable nature of the human spirit. It taught me that within each of us lies the capacity to face our darkest hours and emerge transformed - to take the experiences that threaten to break us and use them as fuel for our regeneration.

This hard-won wisdom has become the bedrock of my life philosophy, a reminder that no matter how bleak the circumstances may seem, there is always the potential for growth, reinvention, and triumph over adversity. I now seek to impart this unshakeable belief in the transformative power of resilience to others, inspiring them to embrace their trials and forge their paths to a brighter, more purposeful future.

Yet, through it all, I refused to give in to despair. I knew that my journey, however tumultuous, was far right, illuminating a path forward even when the darkness threatened to consume me.

-Shock and Awe

Five people were before me when I entered my office and conference room. I had no idea who they were. I'd come back for a meeting to talk about a trade show, and these people in there introduced themselves and said, please sit down, which I did, and it explained to me that my wife was divorcing me, and they gave me the paperwork, and they shuttled her out of the room. I was in shock, and then they told me I had to leave, which I did. I went back to my condo."In that darkness, As I sat in the suffocating darkness of that moment, the very idea of rebuilding seemed like an impossibility - a distant dream forever shattered by the all-consuming pain and overwhelming sense of betrayal that engulfed me. But now, with the clarity of hindsight, I can see that this breaking point was, in fact, a crucial catalyst for transformation. The fire forged me; my old life forced me to confront the deepest recesses of my being. In questioning everything I thought I knew about myself and my place in the world, I unearthed a wellspring of strength and resilience I had never imagined. As I began the arduous process of piecing together the fragments of my shattered existence, I came to understand that true resilience is not about sidestepping adversity but rather, staring it down unflinchingly and allowing it to reshape you into something more substantial, wiser, and more authentic. I left the office.

"Mere moments later, a thunderous knock reverberated through the door, heralding the arrival of Boston police officers bearing a restraining order that compelled my immediate departure from the premises. I had to leave the condo, so after 35 years, it was done. I left, went to my garage, got my car, and drove to Wellesley to talk to an attorney friend who told me that if you have a restraining order, you better stay away. They will put you in jail. "Go find a place to stay and call me." That night, I stayed in my car the next night. I stayed at my sister's, then moved to my brother's in Rye, New Hampshire. I was distraught, lost, and crying. I was in utter shock.

-Background for story

So what happened to me? I came back from a meeting in Burlington, Mass, and went to my office in Boston, pretty excited. I just got a commitment to do a crowdfunding for live-screen TV. Crowdfunding was new then, and I found a group willing to take a shot and raise capital. Live screen TV was designed to be the truth for anybody to go live streaming; the more credible their reporting or content, the more audience they would get, and the more we would monetize both provider and viewer. That was the plan!

I was rudely taken out of my Boston life. Everything I was doing was now dead in the water, and I honestly had to start my life again. This is probably the second and third biggest shock in my life as my dad's death and a few other events that I will watch Watershed events then I can reflect on, but this took the wind out of my sales. I was down and out for three months solid, not knowing what to do and being bewildered. I lost my condo, I lost my car, I lost my business, I lost my family, and I was devastated.

After three months, my brother and sister-in-law, who had taken great care of me, cut me loose and helped me get my place. I moved back to the suburbs of Boston in a modern house that had no insulation, and I froze my butt off for the rest of that winter. I wasn't sure what I was going to do next. I tried to revive my Live TV screen, but I soon realized it was not something I could get done.

I know there are always two sides to every story, and as the newly divorced male in this situation, I had to face a lot of different challenges. One was being accountable for my part in the failure of the marriage. Not only was I in terrible pain, but it mirrored the devastation I had experienced when my father passed away at the young age of 15. I was indeed on the ropes.

Looking back, I understand why the marriage ultimately ended. I had observed the gradual deterioration of our relationship over time. When we moved back to Boston, I suggested it as an opportunity for us to reinvent ourselves without the constraints of raising children. It was a tough adjustment for my wife initially, but once she settled in, we had a good run in the city for the last ten years.

However, that period was not without its struggles. The business had to go through a significant upheaval when we lost our manufacturer in France, forcing us to reinvent that side of the company. The expenses of living in Boston also added immense pressure on both of us. Over time, we simply drifted apart, like so many couples do after being together for 37 years. It was a very tough situation all around.

-Scorched Earth

My divorce was a scorched-earth affair, devastating me to the core. Not only was I emotionally shattered, but I found myself on the brink of losing everything. My ex had retained an attorney who seemed to harbor an intense bias against men, and they worked in cahoots with the judge to ensure I had no chance. In that first session, I was accused of stealing money from my company - an utterly baseless claim that the judge accepted without question. Like that, I was stripped of all financial support and left with a mere $600 in my bank account, my car being the only asset I could still claim.

I had just qualified for Social Security, which would now be my sole means of income, around $1,850 per month. To make matters worse, I had missed the deadline to enroll in Medicare, leaving me with a reduced amount of an extra $30 per month for the rest of my life. I found refuge in a small house in Waltham, where I would remain for a year before meeting my partner, Lucy and moving to Portsmouth, New Hampshire.

The months that followed were some of the darkest of my life. As I grappled with the emotional devastation, a sage therapist offered me a glimmer of hope. "Michael," she said, "you won't like what I say today, but when you look back three years from now, you will appreciate yourself much better. You will be better off." I heard her words, but I did not fully comprehend their meaning at that moment. At the time, I couldn't fully grasp the wisdom in her words. The pain was too raw, the future too uncertain. But as the years have passed, I've understood the profound truth in what she said. As devastating as they were, my challenges during that period ultimately forced me to grow, adapt, and rediscover my strength. Looking back, I can see how each trial has shaped me into the person I am today - more resilient, compassionate, and committed to living life on my terms."

-Reinvention

Amidst this personal upheaval, I found solace in exploring a newfound passion - understanding the experiences of those in assisted living and nursing homes. As a technologist, I recognized the potential for virtual reality to address the profound loneliness residents often face. This sparked an idea to develop a VR app tailored to their needs. However, just as I was getting started, my computer broke down, and I encountered an unexpected savior - a gentleman named Matthew who had the technical skills and the desire to join me on this journey.

Over the next seven years, Matt and I embarked on an incredible odyssey, delving deep into virtual reality, binaural beats, and neuroscience. Simultaneously, we launched RealTView, which leveraged 3D imaging to capture real estate listings. Starting with no capital, just sheer determination and goodwill, the business grew from zero to $240,000 in revenue before the devastating impact of COVID-19.

Throughout this whirlwind of personal and professional challenges, I found solace in measuring my success and celebrating the small victories and accomplishments that may have gone unnoticed by others. The pandemic brought new obstacles, as projects with healthcare giants like Northwell Ventures and Henry Schein were back burnered due to shifting priorities. Yet, I refused to be discouraged, recognizing that the accurate measure of success lies not in the result but in the resilience and growth forged along the way.

-Rude Awakening

Amidst the turmoil of my personal and professional life, I was dealt with another devastating blow: the loss of my mother. She had been a wellspring of love, support, and inspiration, nurturing me through countless trials and triumphs. Her passing left me grappling with a profound sense of emptiness that seemed to permeate every aspect of my being.

The complexity of our relationship, with its intricate web of joys and struggles, only intensified the ache of her absence. It was a stark and painful reminder of the fleeting nature of life, a wake-up call to cherish every precious moment with those we hold dear, for we never know when fate will intervene and leave us to navigate the world without their guiding light. But even amid grief, I found solace in my mother's lessons. Her resilience, creativity, and unwavering commitment to making the world a better place have shaped me in countless ways. I knew the best way to honor her memory was to continue pursuing my passions and purpose with the same dedication and love.

In the depths of my grief, I found myself drawing on the very lessons my mother had imparted throughout my life - the importance of perseverance, the power of love, and the courage to face even the darkest of days with an open heart. As I navigated the uncharted waters of life without her physical presence, I began to understand that her legacy lived on within me, a guiding force that would continue to shape my path and inspire my choices.

Through the pain of loss, I discovered a newfound strength and determination, a resolve to honor her memory by living a life filled with purpose, compassion, and the relentless pursuit of growth. And in doing so, I found that even in the face of the most profound challenges, the human spirit has an extraordinary capacity for reinvention and transformation."

-Technology on Steroids

Another challenge I faced during this period was the rapid pace of technological change and disruption. As an entrepreneur in tech, I was no stranger to the constant evolution of tools, platforms, and business models. However, the sheer speed and scale of the changes in the 2010s and early 2020s was unlike anything I had ever experienced.

From the rise of artificial intelligence and machine learning to the explosion of "big data and the Internet of Things," it seemed like every day brought a breakthrough or a new challenge to navigate. Staying ahead of the curve required constant learning, experimentation, and adaptation, and sometimes, I felt like I was barely keeping my head above water.

But through it all, I remained committed to my core values and vision for the future. I surround myself with talented, passionate individuals who share my commitment to innovation and impact, and together, we worked tirelessly to build products and services that made a real difference in people's lives.

My most exciting venture during this period was re-imagining the use case of our VR app by launching a new platform focused on mental health and well-being. Inspired by finding a solution for people who struggle with anxiety and depression, as well as the experiences of countless others in my network, I set out to create a tool that would make it easier for people to access the support and resources they need to thrive. (as of this publishing, it is still a work in progress)

It is a daunting undertaking, but one that I believe in deeply. With the help of my growing network of partners and investors, I have built a platform that has the potential to make a real impact. It's a constant and powerful reminder of the importance of pursuing projects that align with your values and passions, even amid uncertainty and risk. (I am consistent)

Of course, only some of the ventures during this time succeeded. There were plenty of false starts, setbacks, and failures. However, I learned to view each of these experiences as an opportunity for growth and learning rather than a reason to give up or lose hope. Matthew and I were at the doorstep of 2 Fortune 500 companies when Covid knocked us out of the game. This was a giant accomplishment unto itself!

I also learned the importance of caring for myself and my relationships during stress and uncertainty. As an entrepreneur, it's easy to get caught up in the hustle and the grind to prioritize work over everything else. I realized that true success and fulfillment come from *finding a balance between the professional and the personal, investing in the people and the things that matter most.*

Looking back on this decade, I'm struck by how much I grew and changed as a person and leader. The challenges I faced, both personal and professional, forced me to confront my limitations and develop new skills and strategies for navigating uncertainty and adversity.

However, the most important lesson I learned during this time was the power of resilience and perseverance. No matter how difficult the circumstances or how daunting the obstacles are, I discovered there is always a way forward if you're willing to keep pushing, learning, and believing in yourself and your vision.

As I look ahead to the next chapter of my journey, I do so with a renewed sense of purpose and deep gratitude for the experiences and people who have shaped me. I know that new challenges and opportunities will be waiting around every corner, but I also know that I have the skills, mindset, and support network to face them head-on and come out stronger on the other side.

And so I move forward with excitement and hope, knowing that the best is yet to come and that the journey itself is the ultimate reward. Whether I'm building a new venture, mentoring the next generation of entrepreneurs, or simply pursuing my personal growth and development, I know I'm exactly where I am meant to be, doing exactly

what I am meant to do. (see some more of my books and essays @
www.michaelwberman.com[1]

---

1.   http://www.michaelwbwrman.com

Part IX

Reflections on the Entrepreneurial Journey

When we free ourselves from the shackles of negativity and focus solely on following the rules that serve our highest good, that is when success truly floods our lives.

Of course, navigating the risk-reward landscape is challenging. It requires a keen eye for detail, the ability to anticipate potential pitfalls and the resilience to bounce back from setbacks. But the rewards are beyond measure for those who have embraced this challenge. In mastering the delicate balance of risk and reward, we unlock the keys to building thriving businesses that leave a lasting impact on the world around us. But make no mistake - this is no mere game of chance. Instead, it is a carefully choreographed dance that requires intention, a positive mindset, and the unwavering determination to be the best version of ourselves. It is about taking risks with purpose, understanding our fears, and confronting them head-on through visualization and self-belief.

Far too often, we fall prey to the temptation to compete - to measure our progress against others and constantly seek validation through external means. But the true path to greatness, I've found, lies not in besting the competition but in **striving to be the best version of ourselves.**

1. Confronting the Demons within Overcoming Self-Doubt and Shame

It's common for us to be our own harshest critics, to let self-doubt and shame hold us back from sharing our stories and celebrating our accomplishments. I know this struggle all too well. When my daughter Jennifer first suggested I write this book, my immediate reaction was skepticism - "Why would anyone want to read about my life? It's not that amazing." The voice of shame was quick to surface, whispering that my experiences weren't worthy and that I shouldn't dare to share them. But my daughter's perspective was so different. She saw the richness of my journey and the resilience I had built through both successes and failures. She wanted me to embrace that, to see my worth.

That conversation was a turning point for me. I realized shame is often just an illusion, a limiting belief we impose on ourselves. The reality is that each of our stories holds immense value, no matter how "ordinary" they may seem. Our stumbles and challenges don't make us less deserving of sharing our voices. It's those very experiences that can provide the most powerful lessons and inspiration for others. In reading this book, I hope you'll be encouraged to silence your inner critic, let go of shame, and honor the beauty of your unique path. Your story matters. You matter.

2. In Search of Meaning: Aligning My Entrepreneurial Ventures with My Values

Pursuing a purpose can be challenging. Along the way, I've had to confront the insidious force of self-doubt, that nagging voice telling me I'm not good enough, not smart enough, not capable enough. I've learned that *self-doubt is the biggest killer of dreams,* the most potent obstacle to achieving our goals. The key to overcoming it is to cultivate an unshakeable belief in ourselves and our abilities and to trust in the unique gifts and talents that we bring to the table.

Of course, belief alone is not enough. We must also be willing to face challenges head-on to find the good even in the darkest of times. When I lost everything in my divorce, when *I found myself starting over at 65,* it would have been easy to give in to despair and bitterness. But I made a conscious choice to be thoughtful about my pain, to look for the bright lights amidst the darkness. I found gratitude for the love and support of my family and friends and for the opportunity to reinvent myself and discover new passions and purpose.

3. From Boomers to Zoomers: Uniting Generations in the Entrepreneurial Spirit

As I reflect on my entrepreneurial journey, I can't help but recognize the stark differences between the business landscape I navigated as a Boomer and the realities confronting today's younger entrepreneurs. The digital revolution I fought to stay ahead of has only accelerated, creating challenges and opportunities that would have been unimaginable in my early days.

For starters, the pace of change has become utterly dizzying. When I started, we relied on landlines, fax machines, and printed directories to conduct business. The idea of being constantly connected via smartphones and social media was the stuff of science fiction. But now, Millennials and Gen Z founders are digital natives, fluent in the ever-evolving languages of technology, data, and online engagement.

Access to capital has also transformed. Gone are the days of scraping together funding from personal savings, family, and traditional lenders. Today's young entrepreneurs have many options—from crowdfunding platforms to venture capital firms hungry for the next big thing. The speed at which ideas can be transformed into viable businesses is staggering.

Yet, with these advances come new sets of hurdles. The competition is fiercer than ever, with countless startups vying for attention and market share. The pressure to innovate, pivot, and scale at a breakneck pace can be utterly relentless. And the ever-present specter of disruption looms large, with established players constantly seeking to outmaneuver the upstarts.

In many ways, I am fortunate to have built my foundation in a slightly more analog era. The lessons I learned about perseverance, adaptability, and cultivating genuine human connections have served me well, even as the landscape has transformed. I've had to work hard to stay current and learn new skills and mindsets, but that challenge has kept me young.

At the same time, I can't help but admire the sheer audacity and boundless ambition of today's young entrepreneurs. Their fearless problem-solving, comfort with risk-taking, and innate understanding of digital ecosystems are nothing short of inspiring. They aren't weighed down by the baggage of "the way things used to be," like I sometimes am.

And therein lies the beauty of entrepreneurship across generations. We each bring unique perspectives, experiences, and areas of expertise to the table. Boomers like myself offer hard-won wisdom, a steady hand, and an understanding of the fundamentals. Millennials and Gen Zers bring lightning-fast adaptability, technological fluency, and a vision unbounded by convention.

It's when we can bridge that generational divide, learn from one another, and collaborate in meaningful ways that the true magic happens. The fusion of old-school business acumen and new-school digital savvy, the melding of long-term thinking and laser-sharp agility—that's where the most innovative solutions are born, where the most transformative companies take root.

So, as I continue on my entrepreneurial journey, I'm not just looking to leave a legacy for those who will come after me. I'm also actively seeking ways to mentor, inspire, and learn from the next generation of trailblazers. Ultimately, we're all united by a shared drive to create, innovate, and make our mark on the world.

-Being Present

This brings me to another crucial lesson: *the importance of being present*. So often, we get caught up in ruminating about the past or worrying about the future, and we forget to appreciate the beauty and opportunity of the present moment. The past is gone, and the future is uncertain, but we can shape our reality now. By staying grounded in the present, we can find the clarity and the courage to take bold action towards our goals.

-Setting Goals:- *think big and to think differently*

When setting those goals, I've found that the key is to *think big and to think differently.* Divergent thinking and problem-solving have been essential in my entrepreneurial journey, allowing me to identify unique opportunities and create innovative solutions. Whether it's been setting the vision for a groundbreaking VR app or identifying an untapped market for a real estate imaging business, I've learned to trust my instincts and follow my curiosity wherever it leads.

However, even the boldest vision is only meaningful when it has a strong foundation of planning and execution. Over the years, I've honed a process for setting milestones, conducting market research, and prioritizing customer needs, which has been essential to my success. By *taking a data-driven approach and staying focused on creating real value for customers,* I've built ventures that achieve my vision and make a tangible impact in people's lives.

Ultimately, the most important lesson I've learned is embracing my magnificence. We are all unlimited human beings with boundless potential to create, love, and make a difference. Too often, we let ego, lack, and fear hold us back from pursuing our deepest passions and boldest dreams. But when we let go of those limiting beliefs and step into our power, there's no limit to what we can achieve.

As I look back on my startup journey, from the pain of personal loss to the thrill of new love and new beginnings, I'm filled with deep gratitude and awe. Every experience, lesson, and challenge has shaped me into who *I am today. This person knows that resilience is a choice, that purpose is worth fighting for, and that our most significant power lies in our ability to embrace change and keep moving forward.*

So, to you, dear reader, I offer this final piece of wisdom: trust in your journey. Embrace the twists and turns, the ups and downs, the moments of darkness, and the moments of light. Know that every experience is a teacher, and every challenge is an opportunity for growth. And most of all, know that you are enough to pursue your dreams, make a difference, and leave a legacy that will ripple into the world long after you're gone.

The journey continues, my friends. May you greet each new day with courage, curiosity, and an open heart. May you find your purpose and passion and never give up on yourself. The best is yet to come

-The Last Ten Years

During the last ten years, at the heart of my journey, I have committed to a "Massive Transformative Purpose" (MTP) coined by Peter Diamandis. This is one of the driving ideas that has guided me through every decision and obstacle, the north star that has kept me focused on making the world a better place.

For me, that purpose has been about leveraging technology and innovation to create solutions that enhance people's lives, whether through a virtual reality app for seniors or a platform for empowering content creators. (Read my book "The Baby Boomers Guide to the Creator Economy") I have also been influenced by Joe Dispenza, Bruce Lipton, Greg Bradon, Abraham Hicks, Paula Dweck, Ray Kurzweil and Peter Diamandis, Sam Harris, and so many other brilliant new-age thinkers. (see reading list)

4. Nothing Ventured, Nothing Gained: The Delicate Dance of Risk and Reward

In the high-stakes world of entrepreneurship, perhaps no more vital skill is the ability to navigate the complex interplay of risk and reward. For it is in our willingness to take calculated leaps, to explore the consequences and possibilities that lie beyond our comfort zones, that we unlock the true potential for breakthrough success.

5."The Interplay of Faith and Entrepreneurship: How Judaism Shaped My Journey"

Reflecting on my entrepreneurial journey, I've recognized how deeply my spiritual beliefs and practices have shaped how I approach business and leadership. It's not something I often talk about openly, as I've always believed that one's faith and inner journey are deeply personal matters. But the truth is, the lessons and principles I've gleaned from my lifelong exploration of Judaism, Kabbalah, and other contemplative traditions have become inextricably woven into the very fabric of who I am as an entrepreneur.

At the heart of it is a deep sense of purpose - a conviction that my work must serve a higher calling and make a tangible difference in the lives of those I encounter. This ethos of "tikkun olam" - the Jewish concept of "repairing the world" - has been a guiding light, pushing me to seek opportunities to leverage my skills and resources to uplift others, alleviate suffering, and foster greater connection and well-being.

It's a philosophy that has manifested in diverse ways throughout my career - from the virtual reality app I developed to combat loneliness in senior care facilities to the real estate imaging business that sought to streamline the home-buying process. But at the core, it's always been about finding ways to create value that transcends the bottom line and builds enterprises that are a true force for good in the world.

And this sense of purpose has, in turn, shaped the way I make decisions and lead my ventures. I've always been acutely aware that my choices and priorities profoundly impact the lives of those around me. So, I strive to approach every challenge through compassion, seeking to understand multiple perspectives and find solutions that uplift and empower rather than divide and conquer.

It's a delicate balance, to be sure - blending the practical realities of running a successful business with the loftier ideals of spiritual and ethical leadership. But for me, it's been an essential part of my journey, a way of staying grounded and centered amidst the constant flux and pressure of entrepreneurship.

When I face a difficult decision or the path forward seems murky and uncertain, I often turn to the wisdom of my spiritual practices—the teachings of Kabbalah, the rituals and rhythms of my Jewish faith, and the insights gleaned from contemplative traditions. I can tap into a bottomless wellspring of clarity, discernment, and courage in these quiet moments of reflection and introspection.

And when I've felt most tested and most tempted to compromise my values, this spiritual foundation has kept me steadfast. The knowledge that I am part of something greater than myself and that my actions and choices have a lasting impact has given me the strength to stay true to my principles, even when the more straightforward path might have been to succumb to greed or expediency.

So, as I look back on my entrepreneurial journey, I realize that my spiritual beliefs and practices have been an integral part of who I am and how I lead. They have imbued my work with meaning and purpose, guiding me toward decisions and actions that uplift my interests and the well-being of my community and the world. This integration of the spiritual and the practical will continue to inspire and empower the next generation of entrepreneurs and business leaders. I encourage you to find a personal path that will bring you joy!

"Looking back on my life, I realize that the challenges I faced as a Jewish entrepreneur were deeply intertwined with the social and cultural climate of the times. Growing up in a relatively progressive town like Newton, I still encountered my fair share of anti-Semitism - in school and even within my community. This subtle yet pervasive prejudice was a constant backdrop to my formative years, shaping my awareness of my identity and my place in the world.

However, my connection to my Jewish faith was forged through this adversity, thanks to my father's unwavering commitment. Judaism's rituals, traditions, and spiritual teachings became a vital source of nourishment, equipping me with the tools to navigate the complexities of my identity. As I explored various belief systems over the years, I always found myself drawn back to the wisdom of Kabbalah.

On my road back post-divorce, I was fortunate to meet Rabbi Nechemia Shusterman and his wife Rabitzen Raizel. They unselfishly offered me a profound sense of community and belonging. I am forever grateful to have these fantastic people in my life!

This spiritual and cultural exploration journey has undoubtedly influenced how I approach business and entrepreneurship. The values of justice, compassion, and the inherent dignity of all people have been a guiding light, informing my decision-making and how I treat people.

At times, this commitment to my beliefs has put me at odds with the more cutthroat aspects of the business world, but I've always strived to stay true to my principles, even when it meant taking the road less traveled.

Embracing the social and cultural contexts that have shaped my life has made me a more well-rounded, empathetic, and adaptable entrepreneur. It has taught me to see the world through a lens of nuance and complexity, to seek out diverse perspectives, and to recognize the humanity in all those I encounter, regardless of their background or beliefs. These lessons have been invaluable in navigating the ever-changing business landscape, and I hope that by sharing these insights, I can inspire others to do the same."

Conclusion

"As I reflect on the winding path that has led me to this moment, I'm struck by the profound truth that every experience, every challenge, and every triumph has been a teacher, guiding me towards a deeper understanding of myself and the world around me.

Through the lens of my entrepreneurial journey, I've come to see that resilience, adaptability, and the power of relationships are not abstract concepts but the very foundation of a life of purpose and impact.

Resilience has been my constant companion, the inner strength that has allowed me to weather the storms of personal loss, professional setbacks, and the inevitable failures that come with the territory of building something from nothing. It's the voice that whispers, 'Keep going,' even when every fiber of your being wants to give up.

Adaptability has been my secret weapon, the key to unlocking new opportunities and staying relevant in a constantly evolving world. From the early days of navigating the transition from analog to digital to the more recent challenges of pivoting in the face of a global pandemic, the ability to embrace change and learn on the fly has been the difference between stagnation and growth.

Relationships and connections that have lifted me, pushed me forward and given me a reason to believe in myself even in the darkest times. From my family's unwavering love and support to the mentors who saw my potential before I could see it myself, I've learned that no one succeeds alone. We are all the products of the people who have touched our lives and shaped our paths.

But the most significant lesson is that there is always time to start anew, reimagine what's possible, and chart a new course. My journey is a testament to the transformative power of reinvention, the courage to shed the old stories that no longer serve us and embrace the ones yet to be written.

To you, dear reader, I offer this invitation: Let my story be a reminder that within you lies a wellspring of resilience, a boundless capacity for growth, and a network of support just waiting to be tapped. Embrace the challenges, learn from the failures, and never stop believing in the power of your dreams.

The entrepreneurial path is not for the faint of heart but for those willing to bet on themselves, to take the leap of faith and trust that the net will appear. It's for those who understand that the most significant rewards come not from playing it safe but from daring to imagine a world that doesn't yet exist and having the audacity to create it.

So, here's to the journey: its twists and turns, the highs and lows, and all the iterations in between. Please find your path to resilience, adaptability, and profound connection. And may you always remember that your story, like mine, is still unfolding—a beautiful, messy, glorious work in progress."

"Only he who sees the invisible can do the impossible."
- Frank Gains

About the Author

Michael W.G. Berman is an experienced entrepreneur and pioneer in the creator economy. With a proven track record of launching multiple successful startups, growing and turning around existing businesses, and raising capital, Berman is well-suited to share his insights and lessons from the entrepreneurial journey.

Berman has extensive experience in high-tech industries, focusing on introducing innovative products and services. His business philosophy is centered around the key pillars of sales, operations, process, performance, transparency, tenacity, and a robust entrepreneurial spirit. This approach has enabled him to develop and deliver successful new offerings while providing focused leadership at the intersection of marketing, strategy, and customer experience.

In addition to his entrepreneurial pursuits, Berman also offers consulting services to startups and entrepreneurs worldwide. Leveraging his knowledge and real-world experience in launching and growing successful businesses, he helps other entrepreneurs navigate the challenges of starting, scaling, and evolving their ventures.

Berman's consulting services include business strategy, market research, product development, and fundraising. Known for quickly understanding his clients' unique challenges, Berman provides actionable advice and guidance to help entrepreneurs achieve their goals and drive sustainable growth.

Driven by a passion for empowering others to bring their ideas to life, Berman is respected for his ability to offer insightful, tailored solutions that address the specific needs of each entrepreneur and startup he works with. His clients appreciate his entrepreneurial mindset, breadth of practical experience, and commitment to helping them overcome obstacles and unlock their full potential.

"Only he who sees the invisible can do the impossible."

Stuff I Love

"Only he who sees the invisible can do the impossible." Frank Gaines

"Out of clutter, find simplicity; from discord, find harmony; in the middle of difficulty lies opportunity. Albert Einstein

"Don't promise what you can't deliver" Unknown

"The less you expect, the more you get"- Unknown

"Don't let someone else's limited beliefs stop you."

The 5 C's - Clarity, Creativity, Curiosity, Communication, Critical Thinking

Adversity Reveals Genius- Horace

A Positive Thinker sees the invisible, feels the intangible, and achieves the impossible!

10 Things to Give Up!

1. Excuses
2. Self Doubt
3. Fear of Failure
4. Procrastination
5. People Pleasing
6. Fear of Success
7. Negative Thinking
8. Negative Self Talks
9. Judgment of Others
10. Negative People in Your Circle:

"The entrepreneur always searches for change, responds to it, and exploits it as an opportunity." Peter Drucker

"Entrepreneurs must be willing to be misunderstood for long periods," Jeff Bezos.

"No matter what knocks you down, get back up and keep going. Never give up. Great Blessings are a result of great perseverance."

"You need to understand that life isn't what you're given: it's what you create, what you overcome, and what you achieve, then make it beautiful."

"I am thankful for my struggle because I would have stumbled across my strength without it."

"Be afraid to start all over again. You may like your new story better."

"Smart men don't tell you how smart they are. Rich men don't tell you how rich they are. Tough men don't tell you how tough they are. Honest men don't tell you how honest they are. Only Con men do!"

Quotes by Idowu Koyenikan

"What is considered impossible is someone else's opinion. What is possible is my decision."

"Whenever I am in a difficult situation where there seems to be no way out, I think about all the times I have been in such situations and say to myself, "I did it before so that I can do it again."

"The mind is like a muscle—the more you exercise it, the stronger it becomes, and the more it can expand."

"You can. "When a person knows that all events of his life are for the ultimate good, then life resembles Paradise.

Every human has his or her designated path in life; life's trials, obstacles, and difficulties are designed for our ultimate benefit."

Rebbe Nachman

"You either look at the problems you come across as opportunities or concede to being defeated. Either way, the choice is yours. Do not let your past hold you back from what you think you can achieve in the future." - Einstein

Influential Reading

The Blind Watchmaker, Why the Evidence of Evolution Reveals a Universe without Design by Richard Dawkins,

The Selfish Gene by Richard Dawkins

Global Brain, The Evolution of Mass Mind from The Big Bang to the 21st Century by Howard Bloom

The Genius of the Beast, A Radical Re-Vision of Capitalism by Howard Bloom

The Mohammed Code by Howard Bloom

The End of Faith, Religion Terror and the Future of Reason by Sam Harris

Letter to a Christian Nation by Sam Harris

The Moral Landscape, How Science Can Determine Human Values by Sam Harris

Free Will by Sam Harris

Waking Up, A Guide to Spirituality Without Religion by Sam Harris

Islam and the Future of Tolerance by Sam Harris

A Brief History of Time, The Illustrated, Updated & Expanded Edition by Stephen Hawking

Why Evolution is True by Jerry A. Coyne

Faith vs. Fact, Why Science and Religion are Incompatible by Jerry A. Coyne

Evolutionaries, Unlocking the Spiritual and Cultural Potential of Science's Greatest Idea by Carter Phipps

The Singularity is Near When Humans Transcend Biology by Ray Kurzweil

How to Create A Mind, The Secret of Human Thought Revealed by Ray Kurzweil

Fantastic Voyage by Ray Kurzweil

The Art of the Impossible by Steven Kotler

Stealing Fire Steven Kotler and Jamie Weil

The Biology of Belief by Bruce Lipton

Every Belief is a Lie by Lisa Schermerhorn

The Universal Garden of Emuna By Shalom Arash

God is not Great, How Religion Poisons Everything by Christopher Hitchens

The Biggest Secret by David Icke

Human Race, Get off Your Knees by David Icke

The Creature from Jekyll Island, A Second Look at the Federal Reserve by G. Edward Griffin

None Dare Call It Conspiracy by Gary Allen

It's Not About What Happens to you it's What You Do About it by W Mitchell

The Speed of Trust by Steven M.R. Covey

Drive: The Surprising Truth About What Motivates Us by Daniel Pink

Seven Habits of Highly Effective People By Steven Covey

Switch: How to Change Things When Change is Hard

Combatting Cult Mind Control by Steven Hassan

Going Solo: The Extraordinary Rise and Surprising Appeal of Living Alone by Eric Klinenberg

The Yiddish Policemen's Union by Michael Chabon

The Garden of Gratitude By Rabbi Shalom Arush

The Zohar (English)

Many Other works from the 60'70'80's 90's and 2000's

Don't miss out!

Visit the website below and you can sign up to receive emails whenever Michael Berman publishes a new book. There's no charge and no obligation.

https://books2read.com/r/B-A-HUCPB-EPSMD

BOOKS 2 READ

Connecting independent readers to independent writers.